P9-CRK-535

A LIFE OF LOVELY

OTHER TITLES BY ANNIE F. DOWNS

ANNIE F. DOWNS

A LIFE OF LOVELY

The Young Woman's Guide to
COLLECTING THE MOMENTS
THAT MATTER

PUBLISHING GROUP
Nashville, Tennessee

978-1-4627-9661-8

Published by B&H Publishing Group
Nashville, Tennessee

Author represented by Alive Literary Agency,
7680 Goddard Street, Suite 200, Colorado Springs,
Colorado, 80920, www.aliveliterary.com.

Dewey Decimal Classification: 305.4
Subject Heading: YOUNG WOMEN \ GIRLS \ YOUTH

1 2 3 4 5 6 7 8 • 23 22 21 20 19

To the God I met at Radnor Lake,
the One who found me when
I didn't know I was lost,
the One who makes all things new.

And to my young friend
who will be on the reading side of this page,
I am here for you.

CONTENTS

SECTION 3: WHEN I FOUND LOVELY

A Note from Annie

Dear friend,

I asked some hard questions, that second year of college. Questions about God and myself and what all this was about. About relationships and joy and purpose and money and if this was really how I wanted to be spending my days. Was this life, this life with God, this life that at times seemed to let me down more than I thought a faith life would, really what I was looking for?

My bedroom in that house had no windows, the one deep on the eastside of Athens, Georgia. And I often felt like my questions bounced around my room like plastic balls—never going up to God, never going out to others, never even settling somewhere in myself that felt safe and helpful and good.

I was sad, and figuring all this out felt hard, and I didn't understand what to do. What I didn't know then, that I hope you will learn now, right where you are, is that transformation and suffering come in a pair. I didn't know they would. But the suffering—those questions and hard days—walked me into something I did not know before. And that's what we're going to talk about here.

I have prayed my guts out for you. That you would feel the Holy Spirit stirring in you as you read, not because of me but because of Him. That His voice would be the loudest in your ears and heart and that this little book, a gift from Him to you, would change everything.

When I write books, I always feel like they already exist. It's not my job to create something new; it's my job to find the piece of art God has intended to be shared and put it down on paper. So I call it a gift without hesitation, not because it is a gift from me but because it was a gift to me as well. I hope I found it as God intended it to be found.

Just a note: some names have been changed, some tiny details shifted, to protect those I have loved, do love, and could maybe love in the future. (You never know.)

Thanks for walking this with me. In some way I feel you here with me as I write, and I hope you feel that I'm there with you as you read, just your friend, across the table at a coffee shop, swapping stories and sharing hope. I want to be there with you. It's for you, after all, all this digging and finding and creating. God has something for you here. I can't wait to see what it is.

Sincerely,

Introduction

Have you ever seen a thunderstorm from the window seat of an airplane? I was flying from Atlanta to Dallas recently, and there, in 17F, I saw the storm to our right, just out my window. The dark, brooding, billowing clouds danced along beside us, the darkest of grays, the strangest of purples—the kinds of colors reserved for only the most wicked of storms. And as we flew parallel with it, I saw sheets of rain drenching the innocent souls below. (Bless them, as we say in the South.) The farm landscape looked like patchwork—one area soaked by the storm, then a dry tract of land and city between, then another region dark and wet. Lightning bolts snaked down out of the sky, and I seriously thought about telling the pilot what I had just seen because clearly THAT IS WHY YOU HAVE ME HERE IN 17F, AIRLINE PILOT, TO KEEP AN EYE ON THE WEATHER.

It was like watching a play, where all the characters were interacting, and I just got to enjoy the show from ten thousand feet above.

From my view? It was awesome, actually. But little is beautiful about sitting under a drenching rain, especially if you have plans for your day or if you lack a roof over your head. But to be next to it? To watch nature move at its ever-changing clip and have a fuller understanding of the landscape and what weather does to it? It was beautiful.

I'm not as good at seeing beauty in the thunderstorms of my life as I am from seat 17F.

I typically sit smack underneath them, watching as my clothes are getting soaked and my straightened hair is getting ruined and what I thought was going to happen with my day (my life?) is getting thwarted. And I find no beauty in that.

Have you made any plans lately that didn't go, you know, as planned? Any relationships that fizzled out? New Year's resolutions that didn't make it past February? What about a major that seemed like a perfect fit, but ended up feeling like a dead end?

I get it. I really do. I know what it feels like when everything falls flat (including your meticulously styled locks). It frustrates me, it angers me, it annoys me. I look skyward and wonder what I have done to deserve this lot in life. And when I see ugly on the outside—whether it is my body or my circumstances or the hurt in the world, the processing in my heart isn't much better—and the storm from out there usually ends up inside me.

And it is ugly.

I've been struggling with this my whole life: looking for the beautiful amid the rain, confusion, hurt, and ugly.

My story might be a lot like yours—the mirror has lied, and the enemy has whispered for years, and now we can't look at ourselves and find anything lovely, whether it is raining or not. I have looked desperately. And I've given up. Over and over again. My search has often left me teary, angry, and eating something I regret later. (Thank you, 11:00 p.m. trip to the grocery store for M&M'S.)

I need beauty. I need to see the lovely in my every day. I crave it. Maybe because I have felt it missing in me—in my heart—for so long. Whenever something beautiful is in my sight, I want to devour it. I want to breathe it in, hold it, swallow it, keep it.

But what is it? What is *beautiful*?

We know we are lacking something, like those dry patches of earth that the rainstorm had just missed. But do we know what we're looking for? Would we know what beautiful looked like if we found it? Is it a rainstorm or a new dress or a plate of shrimp and grits or Monet's lily pads?

Yes. It is all of those things. And more. So much more.

For many days in 2011 and the first half of 2012, I found myself writing *grace* in cursive across my left wrist. My life was moving at an incredible speed with work, travel, writing, and speaking, and trying to keep up wasn't going great. I felt alone, I felt worn down, I felt stretched too thin, mostly by my own decision-making. Just tired. Grace was what I was lacking—toward myself and other people and my schedule. And probably, if I'm really honest, I needed to better reflect God's grace by trusting His plan for my life.

Are you okay with me admitting that? I just had reached a point where I was frustrated and worried, and I looked up a lot with a "what have You gotten me into" look on my face. I hope you find that encouraging, not discouraging. Don't think, "Whoa, if Annie can't get it together, how will I?" It's true, I've logged a few more years in life than you, but I've found it still takes work in every stage of life to keep trusting. To keep looking to our God who has the master plan and is working all things out for our good even when I'm only seeing a tiny corner of His masterpiece.

So during those days, every morning I would take my black pen and carefully write *grace* across my left wrist so that as I was driving or waiting somewhere, I could look down and remember the word by which I was to behave. When it's right there on your arm, there isn't much opportunity to be anything else.

At the end of the summer of 2012, that word *grace* marked some important shifts for me. It had been a hard summer. I had just gone to Scotland for two weeks (a place I tend to run to, as we'll discuss later), and a man I was interested in had just made clear we were never going to be a thing. Or, better stated, he said we would always be just friends, and that's not the label I desired. I was surprised and disappointed and angry at myself for hoping.

Grace. I needed it. I felt it ushering me into a new season and a new calling.

Words are my favorite of all the love languages; and this one *grace* meant a lot to me and spoke to me about God and His heart and how I should treat myself and other people. I needed it to seep into me and define me.

Grace reminds me less of who I am and more of who I want to be.

I'm a pretty staunch traditionalist when it comes to writing the first chapter first and the last chapter last, so here we are. At the beginning. Both of us, you and I, are starting this journey together. Toward what? I know, that's a great question.

I think we're walking toward freedom. I think we're walking toward hope. I think we're walking toward the person we really want to be.

So, as I tend to do, I must confess that I'm not always great at living this life of lovely, at persevering when things get hard, or rejoicing in my sufferings. I wish I could write a book from the vantage point of the expert telling you how to live your life, but that's not me. (This is my fifth book, and I've never once gotten to write a book about something I'm good at—just my struggles and weaknesses. That's so annoying. WHEN DO I GET TO

WRITE A BOOK ABOUT HOW TO FOLD A FITTED SHEET . . . because I'm seriously an expert.)

I want to be right there with you, holding your hand, walking through the pain with you, searching out the lovely with you. It wasn't that long ago, really. I can tell you things get better. Not always easier, but better. It's a journey, this life. And I guess I'm hoping this conversation will help both of our journeys because we are taking it together.

My last couple of years have been deeply intense and full of learning and walking and experiencing this need to endure, but I certainly haven't mastered perseverance. I'm just naturally a quitter, not a finisher.

I've spent a lot of time lately in the first part of Romans 5:

Not only so, but we also rejoice in our sufferings, because we know that suffering produces perseverance; perseverance, character; and character, hope. And hope does not disappoint us, because God has poured out His love into our hearts by the Holy Spirit, whom He has given us.
—Romans 5:3–5 NIV

Before these last few years, I thought HOPE was like GRACE. I thought *hope* was a word we hung up in our houses and willed ourselves to have. I used to think hope was a gift from God in its singular form—like love, peace, patience, any of the fruits of the Spirit. But hope isn't a fruit of having a Spirit-filled life. Look at the list in Galatians 5:22–23. No hope mentioned there. What Paul says in Romans, and what I know from my life, is hope is an expensive commodity, not easily won, always fought for, and the result of a process that may take some time.

(That WILL take some time.)

So relax a little. You're not there yet. But know that every struggle, every trial, every day that seems like it will never end is producing something beautiful in you.

I want you to finish what you start. I want you to grow into the kind of woman that is absolutely full of hope to where it overflows and splashes on your people. But that comes at a cost. And I hate to tell you this so early in the book because I don't want you to quit reading, but if you want to be full of hope, you have to suffer a bit. You have to find purpose in the suffering so you don't give up. You have to persevere. And when you persevere, your character, your tested faith and tried integrity, grows. And then hope. Hope arrives.

(And by suffering I don't necessarily mean you have to experience some catastrophic tragedy in your life. You may. Or you may just feel broken. Messy. Unable to move forward. I think we could all benefit from not measuring our suffering against the next person's. Your story is your story. My story is mine.)

I imagine you've already met the suffering requirement at this point in your life. If not, I know you will. But the suffering isn't even the hardest part. It's that perseverance part, isn't it? It is for me. I can figure out how to look at a hard moment in my life and muster up the will to rejoice in it. I can feel when my character is being tried and tested and growing. But perseverance? No bueno.

Ever since people started reading my book, *Let's All Be Brave*, I get a lot of e-mails with the same theme. "I'M GOING TO DO THE THING, ANNIE," they tell me. "I HAVE A DREAM, AND I AM CHASING AFTER IT, AND I'M GOING TO BE BRAVE EVEN THOUGH I'M SCARED."

(They don't always write in all caps, but it sometimes feels like they are yelling with excitement, so I read the e-mails in all caps.)

But my worry is that six months in, they are going to quit. Something is going to get hard, a door is going to close, a whisper of doubt will creep in, a challenge is going to come along. And instead of staying the course, trusting they are on the right path, even if the path doesn't make sense, they will quit.

Abandoned dreams are a heartbreaker to see. Unfinished journeys, where the real joy is just over the hill you never climbed. Those are the broken moments folks lay in bed at night, think about, and regret.

I have some of those.

I don't want any more.

And I want you to have as few of those abandoned dreams as possible. Oh sure, you'll have some. Everyone does. But my honest prayer is that you can set the way now that will take you on the path of least resistance. Or at least when you do meet pain, you'll have the tools in hand to walk through it. To come out on the other side knowing it was worth it. I want to help you lay down some well-worn tracks that you'll travel so many times that when that next trial comes along your brain will know, yes, this is the way. The way of perseverance that leads to character that leads to hope.

I want you to be branded by perseverance; I want it to be a marker of who you are and what you are known for. And what's amazing as a young woman at this stage of your journey is that, at least to some extent, you get to decide. You get to look ahead to the big, scary unknown and say, "This is the kind of person I want to be." I want people to come to you when times get hard and ask you how you always seem to have a right perspective on things.

I want all of that for me too.

I want us to learn to look for the lovely all around us and collect it, hold it close, and see how God drops beautiful things into our lives at just the right time to help us step forward on our own paths.

I'm honored to be here with you. I can't believe I'm the one God trusted with this work, the work of learning to craft a life you will love, pressing into the hard on behalf of the hope, and writing about it. But I believe we were meant for this journey.

-Section 1-

When Lovely Is Lost

Quitter

One of my favorite weekends of all time was when two of my best friends from Edinburgh, Scotland, Harry and Esther, came to visit me in Nashville. It was the stuff dreams are made of. I had approximately fifty-two hours to show them my life and my people and my town. And whether I liked it or not, I had to factor in a few hours for sleep. So drop that fifty-two down to about forty. I wanted them to see so many places: the deliciously historic Loveless Café, Portland Brew in 12th South (my coffee shop of choice), Radnor Lake, Bluebird Café, Country Music Hall of Fame, Cross Point Church . . . the list went on and on. And with only two lunches and two dinners to work with, how would we EVER get to all the restaurants I was dying to show them?

So I narrowed it down. My best couple friends, Annie and Dave, offered to host a dinner in their home so Harry and Esther could meet my nearest and dearest Nashville friends. One dinner gone. I insisted one meal be barbeque because, hello, it's the South. And obviously we went to Martin's on Belmont because it smells like barbeque from 1990 in there, and it is so nostalgic and purely delicious. I wanted their clothes to absolutely reek of hickory smoke. For our second evening's dinner, we looked over the menus of two of the best restaurants in town, and they picked Husk, a farm-to-table restaurant that specializes in Southern cuisine.

It was going to be a perfect night. Late dinner at Husk, then we'd walk from there to Broadway because Harry really wanted to see the honky-tonks. (Who can blame him? It's a fascinating sight . . . more the other patrons than the buildings themselves, but thank you, tourists, for being a great sideshow.) Both sides of Broadway are lined with neon-signed honky-tonks (cowboy language for "awesome places to see live music"), each with their own talented band. Robert's Western World will give you that old-school country music you imagine seeps out of every crevice of Nashville. The Stage offers a louder experience, with the band playing the top country songs currently popular on the radio. All up and down the street, there are restaurants and venues to choose from to suit every live music desire you can muster.

Locals rarely frequent downtown, but when friends come to visit or a birthday party needs a next stop (a last stop?), we have been known to two-step at Robert's. So when my Nashville friends got wind of us going to the honky-tonks with two Scottish newbies, everybody was in.

Until it started to rain.

As Harry and Esther and I devoured an amazing feast at Husk, my iPhone began to buzz with text messages. One after another, each of my dozen or so friends who were planning to meet us out decided to stay in. Harry was befuddled.

"Because of the rain?" he asked.

"Yeah," I said apologetically, "I mean, maybe we postpone and go downtown tomorrow night? Let me check the weather." And I began fumbling through my phone looking for the weather app.

"No. We're going tonight! Why let a little rain stop us?" Harry insisted.

To be fair to my friends who bailed, it *was* a deluge of rain. But to Harry? It was just a speed bump. He wasn't about to let some water keep us from having fun.

Harry wouldn't let a little rain ruin our night because he always deals with a little rain. Scottish people handle rain better than most because it is a daily occurrence. It may only be for thirty minutes, or it could be an afternoon full of showers, but the people who live there know it's coming and are always prepared with an umbrella or a raincoat. Nothing ugly about it.

Before we even finished eating our dinner, the rain had subsided. Although the air was thick with humidity as only a Southern summer night can be, we walked downtown, soaking in the city's lights and sounds until our feet would no longer carry us.

It was beautiful.

Harry is not a quitter. It's one of my favorite things about him. He doesn't let rain stop him or midnight slow him down (though I was losing steam); he goes forward with his plan. Weather doesn't interrupt his life.

That attitude reflects in his personal life, his business life, and his honky-tonk life (apparently).

Me, on the other hand? I'm a quitter.

I feel embarrassed writing all of this, but I just have to tell you the truth. I've never been one for finishing strong or finishing at all.

I grew up with a lot of shame. I was about to write that some of it was my fault and some wasn't, but the truth is that it is never a child's fault when they are smothered in shame. If you need to stop reading right now and let that soak in, then do it. I know for me it was suffocating. Satan started early with me, whispering into my ear that things were my fault, that I should be so embarrassed when I made a mistake, and that I wasn't good enough or strong enough to be who everyone else thought I could be or should be. Oh those lies he loves to tell us. When I think back on the times I quit, what I feel most is how heavy the shame was when I would quit.

I've been trying to think of the first time I quit something because it was too hard. One comes to my mind quickly, probably because it lives close to the surface of my heart and replays in my psyche more than it should.

I started playing soccer when I was in the sixth grade. I went to watch my friend Kristen's game for the first time and immediately wanted to be on the team. It was a game that looked fun and even as an eleven-year-old, I knew my legs were strong and I could kick hard. As soon as Kristen's parents dropped me back off at home, I ran in the house and told my parents I wanted to play soccer. PLEASE AND NOW AND PUT ME ON A TEAM. So the next season I started playing for the YMCA, a little recreational league that ended up being my soccer home for all of middle school and high school.

I played stopper and sweeper. For you non-soccer people, that means I stood back with the goalie and attempted to keep the other team from scoring. I'm not a fast runner, but I'm a strong player. My motto was, "I probably won't catch you in a foot race, but if you get near me, you're going to lose the ball."

Can you believe I had a soccer motto in middle school? Sheesh. I have a competitive streak a mile wide that is only rivaled by my justice streak. So, you can imagine I'm a different kind of Annie on the soccer field.

I loved playing soccer. I was built for team. It's how I work best. A few of us going after the same goal. (Literally, in soccer.) And as I headed off to high school, with a handful of spring and fall seasons under my cleats, I was ready to play in the big leagues.

As a freshman at Sprayberry High School in Marietta, Georgia, I was thrilled to learn my rec league coach was also the head girls' soccer varsity coach. I thought that since he started me consistently during our weekend games at the East Cobb YMCA, I would easily make varsity. So I went into the season with lots of excitement.

The first few weeks of practices are called "conditioning." I almost shudder even just typing that word. It's all about building your endurance and strength, two things I didn't have a lot of and didn't have a lot of desire for. And you don't even get to touch a ball. It's just running and strength training. Every day, a lot of running. A LOT OF RUNNING. And I'm not a great runner.

It's not that my legs or lungs couldn't handle it; it's that my mind couldn't handle it. Even as a young teenager, I knew that was my weakness. The muscle that wasn't strong enough for conditioning was the one between my ears.

(Also, at that point in my life, I should mention, I was already overweight and hated my body. I felt huge and slow, even though, looking back at pictures, I was not that much different in size from my teammates. But I felt very different. Tortoise-like.)

One thing about perseverance I'm slowly discovering for myself: your body can do just about anything your mind decides it can do. I think athletes (real ones, not Annie ones) are built this way. I was not.

Toward the end of the first week of conditioning, we began a drill I'll call leap-frog sprints. If you haven't done them before, CONGRATS and DON'T because they are terrible. The entire team lines up and starts to jog at a slowish pace. The last player in line when the whistle blows sprints to the front of the line and is now the leader of the line and the pacesetter. The whistle blows again, the new last player sprints to the front again. And this happens over and over again as the team runs around the track that encircles our football field.

I started toward the middle of the group. The jogging part was hard for me. I could hear in my mind, "You're never going to make this; this is way too hard." (Is it just me that hears voices in my head? Tell me I'm not crazy! Do you hear it? That voice that says, "You can't." "You'll never." "You're not.") Well, as my spot crept closer to the back of the line, the voice grew louder and panic rose in me. *I'll never be able to sprint to the front of this line,* I thought. *I hate this so much.*

(It's been twenty years since this experience, and I'm telling you, I can still feel the whole thing in my guts.)

The whistle blew and it was my turn. I pushed it into high gear and broke out of line, headed toward the front. Tears formed at the edges of my eyes as I realized my fastest sprint was not much faster than what the team was already doing. I got to the front (by the grace of God alone) and was now in charge of the pace. I tried to keep it going, but I was running out of steam. The drill continued and two girls ran up before me, one at a time when the whistle told them to. When our line of joggers passed the coaches standing at the entrance gate to the field and track, I quit.

I left the line and fake limped toward the coaches. I told them something about my knee hurting and something about how I couldn't keep going, and they said okay and told me to stretch by the fence.

The girls kept running for a few more laps as I watched.

I didn't make varsity that year. I did get to play on the junior varsity team that year and continued to play for the rest of my high school career, including varsity as a junior and senior, and I was awarded best defensive player on our team.

But quitting that day as a freshman marked me.

As I'm thinking back now, that one decision set a course for me, more than I ever realized it would. Because even today, as a thirty-something who hasn't played competitive soccer in more than fifteen years, I look back on that moment and wish I would have done it so differently. It feels like a fork in the road that I never get to return to, and I picked the wrong path.

(And before you slam this book shut and run away, don't hear me telling you that one bad decision will ruin your life. You've lived enough life by now to know that there are consequences, repercussions. There is pain. And maybe you've lived enough life to know there's also hope. That you can take the other path. That even when you get off course, it's not impossible to right the ship. That's why I'm having this conversation with you. Because, I don't want you to quit. I want you to persevere.)

I still wish I hadn't quit that day. What if I had pushed my mind past the place where it said all the things I couldn't do? What would have been different about my soccer career, my high school experience, my life today, if I had persevered? How would I have seen myself differently in the mirror that night?

I will never know. Which makes me angry and sad, even today.

Because it wasn't just that I quit once. I kept quitting. I could have made myself go back to that fork in the road and take the other path. It wasn't out of reach. One quit didn't have to change the trajectory of my whole life. I let the face in the mirror tell me I couldn't do things. I believed it. I could have gone back out there the very next day. But I didn't.

I kept quitting. From letting an attacking goal scorer buzz past me on the soccer field, to quitting friendships, relationships, diets, exercise plans, commitments to reading the Bible, or praying. You name it, I quit it.

How many times have I promised to have a "quiet time" every day for an entire month only to make it three or four days?

How many times have I signed up for a gym membership only to go for a few months and then never show up again when the weight didn't fall off my body?

How many relationships have I run from because of tension or awkwardness or pain? Instead of being brave and facing the hard moments, I run.

I've never been good at looking past my current pain or suffering and trusting that it will pay off in the future. I think the road has always seemed too long. I listen to the voices I hear TODAY without thinking of the hope tomorrow could hold if I would just push through the uncomfortable parts. So when a situation feels painful or scary or hard, I want out.

➤——————→

Today I feel confusion about a man in my life named Johnny. He's single. I'm single. We like being together, but I don't know what he is thinking or where he is going or where we are going or WHAT IS GOING ON. I seem to pendulum swing between THIS MAN IS AMAZING and THIS MAN CONFUSES ME. And every time I swing toward confusion, I want to let go of the pendulum and fly off into the sunset, like a kid leaving the swing at its highest point. I want to go to Scotland or Atlanta or New York City. Anywhere he isn't.

But it's not him. It's the tension. It's the pain. It's the hard. I want to run from it. I don't want to sit in it or feel it because my brain tells me nothing is beautiful here. I consider multiple cities my home—Nashville, Tennessee; Marietta, Georgia; and Edinburgh, Scotland. So when things go wrong in Nashville, I find myself searching on delta.com for flights to Edinburgh, hoping to get out of here pronto. Or I call my friends in Marietta to see if they are free for the weekend for me to drive down to visit with them. I find ways to run to other places.

Why? Why do I want to run?

A few years ago, there was Matt. Matt and I had only been on two dates, but I was in a bad place and was scared of his feelings and what I might be feeling in return. We met about two weeks before my book *Let's All Be Brave* was due to my editor and proceeded to talk and hang out and go on dates for a month or so. And when I turned in *Let's All Be Brave*, I was an absolute wreck. It had stirred up some painful memories, and the writing pace had been insane, and I honestly just felt like a broken version of myself. Not the humble kind of broken but the literal "something isn't right here" kind of broken.

Matt was awesome. He IS awesome. But pit a new relationship against my broken crazy, and my broken crazy wins every time. We had planned a date for Sunday night because I was headed to the beach on Monday for a few days, and he would be out of town for a week when I returned.

I planned to drive to the beach Monday morning. Matt called earlier in the week, and we made tentative plans for Sunday night. Dinner probably, he said, and then maybe a movie. Or a visit to an art exhibit we were both interested in seeing. Sunday night was on, but the plans would be decided later.

And when we hung up, for whatever reason, I panicked because I didn't know what to do with my feelings. And the broken crazy.

So I jumped on Southwest's website, and I bought a flight to Florida. For Sunday morning. (Just to recap: date planned for Sunday night, so I flew to the beach Sunday morning.)

I spent money I didn't have on a flight and a rental car because I was running away. Yes, I know it doesn't make sense. I told you this is part of the broken crazy.

When I sat down on the plane, it ended up that Dave and Kelli, a married couple who are friends of mine, were in the seats next to me. ("It ended up" could be translated to "God planned it.") I teared up as I told them the story. I was running. I was scared. I was quitting something I actually didn't want to quit, just like that soccer drill, because I wasn't strong enough to finish well.

These friends hugged me and told me it was okay.

And then they told me I needed to see a counselor. I didn't have to fly home, and I didn't even have to fix this relationship with Matt; I just had to fix me.

I've always been pretty hard on myself. I'm not one for physical self-harm but mostly because that wasn't really a thing teen girls did in my day; but the mental self-harm, the self-shaming, and the hateful behavior toward myself has always been a part of my life.

Just writing this makes my guts turn and twist because I'm thinking about you and wondering if you've felt the same way. I wonder what messages you hear when you feel you aren't good enough, strong enough, or pretty enough and you want to quit. Maybe self-harm isn't your thing either. (If it is, can I ask you to do something? Can you put this book down right now and go tell someone? I'll wait right here.)

Maybe you try to fix your pain with relationships. Maybe you try to slather your pain with likes on Instagram. Maybe it's something even more serious like alcohol or drugs. Or maybe you're just like me and you listen to the messages in your head and you believe them so much they become part of you. And you hate that part of you.

A little more than a year ago, I wrote in my journal, "Why can't I quit hating myself?" . . . which is almost funny, considering I can quit everything else.

And that question, the question I can't quit about the hate I can't quit is the one I've been trying to answer ever since.

Ugly

I was tiny in the second grade. I mean, tiny. I remember classmates making comments about it. I remember someone carrying me up the stairs at Blackwell Elementary School after recess and saying something about how easy it was.

In third grade, I wore a huge University of Georgia T-shirt with a belt, like a dress. I had seen a classmate do it, and I thought it looked super cool. (Oh, the '80s.) It's the first time I recall making a brave fashion-forward choice when I knew I was attempting a style that was just not normal and was not guaranteed to work out right. We stood in line outside the lunchroom, and I tugged at the T-shirt, making sure it was long enough to pose as a dress, and I readjusted the belt to make sure it sat just so. But I was small enough to pull it off.

In the fourth grade, I did a presentation in front of my class with my baby sister, Sally, about how to entertain and care for a toddler. She was two at the time, and I showed my classmates how to read a book to a child and how to feed the child slices of

American cheese. Real riveting stuff. My dad videotaped it so we could watch it over and over again.

One day that summer, between fourth and fifth grades, I went downstairs to watch the video. Lying on a beanbag in the cool of our basement playroom, I played the video from just a few months before. The memory of this day is so clear to me that I can still feel my legs stuck against the beanbag because we had the type that somehow always attached to us. My sisters were both in the room—Tatum was just a few years younger than me, and Sally was still a toddler. Some neighborhood friends were over as well. We were all watching together, and I felt pride rise up in me. I had loved that presentation, I loved being the center of attention (shocking no one), and I loved showing my little sister off to my friends in my class, and I was sure it was the finest piece of toddler journalism that ever existed.

"You were a lot smaller then," someone said out of nowhere. "Do you see the difference?"

I hadn't.

But I did now.

Suddenly, in a sentence and in a blink, everything changed for me. There was apparently a size I was supposed to be, and I wasn't it. What I was in fourth grade was okay, but whatever had happened over the summer made my body not okay anymore.

I didn't know what a diet was; at least I don't remember knowing. I was just coming into understanding some things were more beautiful than others, but I didn't put myself on that scale, or any scale for that matter.

I was just Annie.

Until Annie was wrong.

And I finished watching the video with an imaginary blanket of shame draped over me. What I was once proud of, merely minutes before, now I just wished to be over and off the television. I wanted to be alone, to think alone.

At that point the problem wasn't that I thought I was ugly. I didn't put those words around it yet. I just knew there was right, and I was wrong. Whatever I was supposed to be, that video-version of Annie, I wasn't anymore. I was more than, so I was less than.

A year later, as a sixth-grader, I went to my first Weight Watchers meeting with another sixth-grader and her mother. I weighed in at 106 pounds. I don't even remember how long I lasted that first time as a member, but I didn't go to many meetings after that first weigh-in. I quit pretty quickly. But I pretended that I didn't. I wanted people to be proud of me. I figured out praise came when I worked to become the Annie everyone else found beautiful, so I was going for it. I remember lying to my sixth-grade math teacher, telling her I lost four pounds in a day because I wanted her to see I was trying to be the skinny version of me, the fourth-grade Annie, that people liked more. She smiled and nodded, giving me just enough praise to hold my shoulders a bit higher. But it didn't fix me. I didn't lose weight; I gained. And I started to question if things were actually going to get "right" or not.

Those years passed, and they whispered a statement to me I hadn't heard before: I was ugly. I needed to change. My appearance was broken, off, wrong, and I needed to fix it and make it right. Instead of just being Annie, now I had to fix Annie. And fixing Annie was hard, not fun, and I wasn't succeeding.

As my feelings toward myself morphed and got complicated and broken, so did my relationship with food. Food was the enemy . . . and the friend. It was the reason I was here, and I hated French fries for that. But it was also where I went for comfort about my feelings, and I loved ice cream for that. I started dabbling with eating disorders in middle school, but again, because I'm a quitter, I could never really stick it out. I got too hungry to be anorexic, especially during soccer seasons, and I was grossed out by my attempts at bulimia.

So I would just binge. Eat whatever I wanted, whenever I wanted. Whatever it took to feel better, to feel like I could outplay the ugly game, I ate. I would eat too much, and then I would feel guilty and angry and want to punish myself, but I wasn't strong enough or brave enough to actually do it. So I would eat more to not feel the pain.

As a kid, I had just been me; now I was growing to hate me. I was broken and couldn't be fixed; and no matter how hard I tried, I wasn't getting better. I was getting worse. (Thank you, puberty, for seemingly ruining everyone's lives for a few years.)

Ugly chased me. I can see that now. I looked in the mirror with disgust throughout my teen years. I only had a handful of outfits in high school, pretty much wearing the same thing every Monday, then the same thing every Tuesday, and it was like that for the entire week. It didn't matter, I thought. I was ugly, no one was looking at me, so I wore what was comfortable, what covered me, and threw my hair up in a bun. It was a gift for my emotions when my high school decided to require uniforms. Because I was practically doing that myself.

I was sure no one was looking at me anyway. But I knew they were listening.

The only thing I had going for me? My jokes. I had grown accustomed to believing no one thought I was beautiful or found anything lovely about my appearance, but I knew if they took time to get to know me, they would like my personality. If I could get in a conversation, I could usually win people over, even if, as I assumed, they thought I was fat and ugly at first glance.

I had a lot of friends. That part of my soul was still alive and well, the part that loved having as many friends as possible at any one time. (This is still true by the way. Ask anyone who tries to plan my birthday party. The invite list gets ridiculously long because I LOVE MY BIRTHDAY and I LOVE MY FRIENDS and I want ALL THE THINGS TOGETHER.) God made me that way, to love making friends, and that survived somehow, during all the darkness. I often thank God my soul wasn't overtaken by the ugly. While my body and mind suffered, He held my heart, protecting it like the beast prince protects the magical rose in *Beauty and the Beast*. I was committed to my faith, active in the youth group, and truly wanted to be a good Christian.

I loved God. I just hated me.

I had no boyfriends in high school. I went to one dance with a date, but he was my friend's boyfriend from another school, so it absolutely did not count as anything except jewels for his crown in heaven. I had guys who were my friends, even some I thought of as best friends, but none who wanted to date me as far as I knew. (Looking back, I can think of one or two who may have been interested, but my little broken spirit would have never recognized interest from a guy at that point in my life.) There was one boy from a different city who I met on a mission trip, but it fizzled before it even started.

I ping-ponged between fad diets throughout high school. Every major diet you've seen on a commercial, I tried. To no avail. I would lose a little bit, get to a weight, maybe forty to fifty pounds more than I wanted to be, and I would lose steam and quit. And then before I knew it, I would gain back all I had lost and more.

It was a heartbreaking battle I knew was going to be the center of my pain for the rest of my life. What I didn't know, what no one knew, is that my body was suffering from polycystic ovary syndrome, a disease more commonly known as PCOS. My period started weirdly and never normalized to a monthly cycle, and I blamed it on myself—that the way I treated my body was messing up my reproductive system. But the truth all along was that PCOS was causing my body to hold on to weight, have irregular cycles, and just misbehave in general.

So my body and my mind fought on different teams for my entire teenage life. My body trying to tell me a disease was keeping me from the healthiest life; my mind trying to tell my body to get it together or else.

And somewhere, in the corner of me, my soul sat quietly, watching the battle, wondering when rescue would come.

I feel like I'm walking a tightrope here. Please don't read this and think, *Oh, Annie thinks you have to be skinny to be beautiful.* The "rescue" I was waiting for wasn't a number on a scale. In the middle of the battle, I thought it was. I wanted that tangible victory—the prize of being the Annie I used to be, being the Annie others thought I should be. What I needed even more than the prize was the journey itself.

But let me also tell you that our bodies aren't somehow disconnected from this journey we're on. God didn't make us spirits or talking heads. He gave us a physical, human body— warts, bumps, lumps, and all. And taking care of that body is part of perseverance. We'll get a new one someday, hallelujah, but until then we make the most of the one we have. That means keeping it in good shape. Not a "shape" that society thinks it should be, but a healthy shape that lets our bodies do what they're supposed to do, which is carry us through this life and be a vessel for God to use.

In college I started to turn toward the whispered lies and look them in the face, giving my soul a voice to stand up for the truth. Beginning that day on the beanbag as a nine-year-old, I just swallowed every thought that came into my head. I didn't question anything; I just believed it. If I heard I was ugly, I was. If I heard I was a failure, a quitter, a letdown, or unlovable, it was probably true. I spent a lot of time in college wrestling through counseling appointments and discipleship meetings with my mentor, working hard to change my mind and believe truth about who God said I was, not what I heard in my head.

My mind began to change, but my body never did. No matter how much I dieted or worked out (always for short stints—my best friend Candace and I called it my "seasons of self-improvement"), I remained overweight. Painfully so. Not knowing about PCOS, I just thought I was a failure.

I won't bore you with the year-to-year recaps, but let me just summarize by saying I continued to fight this battle for another decade after college. The lies came in, sometimes like a tiny stream of water, sometimes like a raging river. I would diet, lose some weight, and then quit, causing the scale to rebound with gusto. I worked hard to say kind things to myself, to speak life and love to myself and my body, but at the root of everything, the hate was still there. Being diagnosed at twenty-two with PCOS felt like a relief, but it didn't change my body like I thought it would.

I was still me. I was still ugly. And no matter how hard I tried, I could not go back to being innocently nine years old and carefree about my form or my food intake. But I think that's what I always wanted. Maybe it wasn't that I wanted to be skinny or beautiful; maybe I just wanted to be free.

Addiction

I'm an escape artist of sorts. When things feel too painful or seem too hard, I escape. Sometimes it looks like a flight to Florida but only when I'm feeling REALLY QUITE DRAMATIC. (Bless you, Matt, bless you.) Often my escape tactic is way simpler than that. A nap. A book. A bowl of ice cream. A movie. Television.

And it's not all bad. In fact, I'd say escaping isn't always bad. We need rest for our bodies, minds, and souls. So a bowl of almond milk ice cream isn't the problem; it's what is going on in my mind and heart as I devour said almond milk ice cream.

I love watching television, not just because it takes my mind somewhere else but mainly just because I actually really enjoy watching it. I've got my shows I watch with the girls on a weekly basis. I've got the old series like *Gilmore Girls* and *The Waltons* that I cannot quit, and give me a Food Network cooking competition, and I'll give you my hour. I've got my guilty pleasures, too, most of which reside on the Hallmark Channel.

(Yes, Hallmark Channel, I cannot quit you. Your hyperemotional love stories set in the Wild West or the constant drama in a small picturesque town off the coast of Seattle are like a flame, and I am a moth. It's your shows. It's your movies. All of it. I'm smitten, and I don't care who knows it.)

I love reality television in some of its forms, namely dating shows, and I'll watch just about any sport you put on my screen. Soccer and football are my top two, but if I need a nap, golf is the sport of choice.

A few years ago I got a kick out of watching the reality shows on A&E. *Hoarders* was like nothing I had ever known (except my grandfather's house). I could watch episode after episode of that show and never tire of the ways people absolutely fill their homes to overflowing with what? Brooms, boxes, cats, clothing, old food, DOLLS. Oh y'all, the doll episodes. Nightmares. They will cause nightmares. Houses where you can't see the floor or walls because of stacks of dolls and doll clothes and doll paraphernalia. It gives me the shivers just thinking about it. And I usually would find a way to fill a bag for Goodwill after watching a few episodes. My brain said, "WATCH OUT, ANNIE, THAT COULD BE YOU."

Another show from A&E I love is *Intervention*. It's such a beautiful, full-circle kind of show. You meet the addict, meet his or her family, look at pictures from the addict's childhood, then watch as the addict is followed by cameras, indulges the addiction, and falls deeper into it. Somehow, every episode, the addict doesn't realize an intervention with family and a therapist is about to happen. Drug users and alcoholics are featured mostly. The beauty of the show isn't the demise of the people (clearly) but in the redemption that comes at the end. The show often provides a one- to two-minute update as the hour is closing. The addict has clearer eyes, usually has gained a bit of healthy weight, and has clean hair. The addict hugs a family member and talks about how hard, but good, their time in rehab was.

When my friend Laura and I lived together in Nashville, we watched a lot of *Intervention*. We would DVR it, recording piles of episodes, and then when we wanted to binge, she would microwave vegetables, and I would pop popcorn, and we'd settle in for a few hours of addiction and redemption.

Laura and I could both relate to the people in the stories, each in our own way, though neither of us has ever been addicted to drugs or a raging alcoholic. But between episodes we would discuss what we thought; we connected it to our lives, and in some instances a character would remind us of people we knew.

I remember one particular episode about a bald man in his mid-forties. He was addicted to cocaine. He did something I had never seen on a previous episode. Sitting in front of a white background, looking straight into the camera, he began to talk about his feelings toward cocaine. He was a little off center from the camera, but his blue eyes bore into the lens and were almost impossible to look away from. He was brutally honest about the drug. He talked about cocaine like a friend he didn't want to have but didn't know life without. He said he wished he could live without it, that he never saw the addiction coming. As soon as he finished a line of coke, he said, he hated himself for it and yet wanted another. He went on and on, and my mouth began to open slowly in shock.

There with my popcorn bowl and Laura right beside me, I began to cry. Not by choice but in a way that was my soul reacting, not my body. Tears flowed down my face faster than I could wipe them away, so I just quit trying. He had just said all the things I didn't know how to say, but I knew exactly what he meant.

Every word.

I felt it deep in my soul, in my high school memories, in my college struggles, in my dinner decisions the night before.

For him it was cocaine. For me it was food.

He defined my addiction.

Every feeling he had toward the drug he hated, I had toward items in the grocery store. It was what I thought was the source of my problems for decades, and yet I could not survive without it. When he looked at me through the television screen and spoke about cocaine, I felt like he was actually saying my own emotions to me.

I fell apart. The tears wouldn't stop. Laura looked like a deer in headlights.

"I'm so sorry," I said, "I don't know what's going on."

But I did.

I had an addiction. For over twenty years I had taken all the pain and hurt and pushed it straight down my throat. For as much as I read the Bible, sat in Sunday school, and made the church my second home, I wish I'd understood, "His ears are open for their cries for help" (Psalm 34:15). Instead of feeling any of the suffering, instead of pressing through the pain and taking it to God, trusting that He heard me, I escaped to anywhere that would feed me, and I stuffed my emotions down by covering them in layers of food.

What if I had found cocaine instead of candy? What if I had drunk beer instead of milkshakes?

I think about it a lot.

I have the same propensity as any other addict; it's just my drug of choice is food.

It's a funny thing, addiction. The very thing we think is freeing us is keeping us a slave. The very thing we think is relieving our pain is actually the thing making us hang on to our suffering. I've seen it take many forms in the lives of young women I know. Sometimes it's the guy that she knows is no good, but she can't let go. She goes back to the relationship time and time again like that little persistent moth to the flame that eventually will swallow her alive. So often it's the blue light of your smartphone telling you someone's thinking about you. Someone is paying attention.

Can I ask you an honest question here before we get too far into this journey? Is there something you're hanging on to that's weighing on you right now like a sack of bricks? Maybe you haven't ever called it an addiction. "Oh it's just this thing I do . . . once in a while . . . once a week . . . every day . . . multiple times a day." If nothing comes to mind, that's okay. Rejoice and keep reading.

But if so . . . I truly believe God wants to do something beautiful with your pain. I'm not telling you, "Hang on; it'll get better." In fact, it's just the opposite. I'm telling you your pain is the very thing that will help you learn to hope. But I'm getting ahead of myself.

There's one nutritional counselor in Nashville that everyone knows. Well, once you start saying out loud you have a problem and need help, all fingers point in one direction: Trisha. I had friends seeing her for eating disorders, which I was sure I didn't have because I had quit them every time I tried, and friends seeing her for nutritional support after some type of injury or surgery.

I called her. "Um," I stumbled into her voicemail box, "my name is Annie, and I think of food like drug addicts think of cocaine. Call me back when you can."

And she did. I cried through our entire first appointment. I never got on a scale, she didn't tell me what to eat or what not to eat. She just looked at me compassionately yet sternly and said I had disordered eating, whether I wanted that label or not, and that this was a real thing. We talked about hurt and pain and memories and food, and then my hour was up and I left.

Trisha felt like a gift from God. Like He saw my suffering, saw my little soul sitting in the corner looking for rescue, and sent a curly-headed counselor to save the day. Or the Annie, as the case may be.

The view outside her office window was really beautiful. The couch where I nestled myself each week faced that window. Looking across the Green Hills area of Nashville, I often would watch the puffy clouds move or rain pour or the sun set during my appointment. Trisha sat right in front of the window, so as I looked at her and listened or looked her way to speak, I also got to see the beautiful outside.

As we continued to meet, she did begin to instruct me on particular foods to stay away from, for my body and for PCOS and for my soul, and some to increase. (Vegetables. Always vegetables. Sigh.) As much as I liked her, often as my appointment got closer, I would consider canceling. If I hadn't done what she asked, or if I just plain didn't want to talk about FOOD, I would scroll to her name in my phone and prepare a quitter's text.

But I always thought about that view out the window. *Show up, Annie,* I would think, *so you can see what's out the window today.* A couple of times that view saved me, as our conversation would pull me from a pit of my own addiction. I would watch the traffic ebb and flow like water. I'd see the sun set behind Green

Hills Mall, turning the sky one hundred shades of evening, or watch as the humans crossed from here to there across sidewalks and parking decks. It was the tiny bit of lovely that helped me hang on and show up. God was doing a big work. I knew it, I just had to keep showing up, even when it hurt or felt hard or wasn't AT ALL what I wanted to do.

The view out that window seemed to me the only thing beautiful in the whole situation, and it was the view that kept me from quitting.

A life of Lovely

I make my living with words. I tell stories about my life and the lives of the people around me (with their permission, of course) in the hopes that someone listening will relate with some aspect of my own story and connect it to their story. At times, as a professional storyteller, I have to expose the really messy parts of my life—like the broken crazy—because I believe someone needs to hear it. I believe stories speak to our hearts.

One thing I love so much about Jesus is that He was also a storyteller. Jesus often presented some of His most important teachings in story form. Of course, He knew what I know—that stories speak to our hearts. Every advertising company in the world knows this. Think about the commercials you see during the Olympics. You can tell me all about the Olympics and the difficulty of the individual competitions and the level of athleticism it takes to get there, and I'll tune you out soon enough. But show me the gymnast who never knew her parents growing up; the downhill skier who suffered injury after injury but fought her way back for one more run; the sprinter who spent his childhood in a refugee camp not knowing where his next meal would come from. Tell me that story, and I'll glue myself to the couch and tune in with popcorn and tissues in hand. (I love the Olympics, but you know I also do not miss a single minute of the World Cup every four years. Praise hands for international sporting competitions being on television worldwide.)

Jesus knew how to connect to people with stories. He told one about the wise and foolish builders. If you went to Sunday school at any point in elementary school, I'm sure you heard it. It goes like this:

> *As for everyone who comes to me and hears my words and puts them into practice, I will show you what they are like. They are like a man building a house, who dug down deep and laid the foundation on rock. When a flood came, the torrent struck that house but could not shake it, because it was well built. But the one who hears my words and does not put them into practice is like a man who built a house on the ground without a foundation. The moment the torrent struck that house, it collapsed and its destruction was complete.—Luke 6:47–49 NIV*

Since you've most likely heard this story before, I'm going to point out three words that ring out loud and clear to me in this passage. The man who put his house on the strong foundation is the one who DUG DOWN DEEP. I love that.

The shallow, sandy stuff on the surface wouldn't do. He had to dig down deep to get to the good stuff that would last. Storms would come, no doubt, but that house would hold. The foundation was sturdy.

Remember that frantic Sunday morning when I hopped on a plane to the beach, flying with my friends, running from the boy named Matt? I finally made it to Florida, but, don't worry, I had packed all my broken crazy. As I drove the rental car to the above-garage apartment in WaterSound where I would be staying, I thought about Dave and Kelli telling me I needed counseling. I could feel things were off—clearly—but I just thought I might be tired and needing a break from my life, more than anything else.

Sheesh, I thought, *I already see Trisha, now I need ANOTHER counselor?* I wasn't sure my finances or my calendar could handle the added strain of an additional appointment. But I trusted them, and so I texted a few friends whom I knew had spent some time in therapy, asking for a name of someone they recommended.

"Jennifer, I've already told you to see her; here's her number" came back a text from a trusted friend. Sitting upstairs on the window seat of the beautiful garage apartment, with a view of the beach and ocean beckoning me to come lie down and think and read, I dialed her number.

"Hi, my name is Annie Downs. A friend gave me your number. Something is kinda wrong with me. I'm sure it's no big deal, but I think I need to talk to someone about it."

I wanted healing. I wanted freedom, relief, change. Something. I needed the broken crazy to go away, and I needed to find the real Annie. The nine-year-old Annie was never coming back, but could I find a healthy adult version of me, with all my past and all my present?

I hoped so. And I was going to dig down deep to find out.

I feel like God has given me a couple of songs to sing with my life. I have to live them first, mind you, but then the choruses seem to just keep repeating. No matter how many stages I stand on or how many conversations I have or how many books I write, a few common themes come out.

1. GOD MADE YOU ON PURPOSE.

We'll talk more about this as we go, but this is a baseline truth you have to believe. It is a pillar of our faith, especially for women. And the sooner you can get this pillar in place, the better. It may never have been said to you like that before, but trust me when I say it is absolutely true. If you don't believe the way you are is God-made and God-loved, the good and the bad, the tight and the flabby, the strengths and the weaknesses, you are missing out on connecting with God on a level that only comes to those who embrace and love His creations. (And that includes you.)

You're different. Whether you call yourself that or you tend to believe you can just fade into the background, you are different. And you don't have to dress a certain way or hang with a certain crowd or collect any accolades to prove it. You are unique. You are the only you there is. God did that on purpose. There are people who see you and see your life and because of the ways you remind them of God, they see Him too. But they see Him differently because of you than they do because of me. It doesn't add pressure for us to be perfect (because I am not), but it just reminds me that I'm put together differently from you. And that's okay. And that's good.

The things you want, the things you love, the things that make you cry, and the things that make you laugh, and the things that make you more angry than you thought you could be—it's a rare combination. In fact, it's a one-of-a-kind combination. Because God made you that way. On purpose.

Your looks. Your loves. Your losses. They are you.

2. GOD MADE YOU TO BE BRAVE.

We were never meant for a wimpy life. Now don't hear me saying we weren't meant for a simple life or a quiet life or a famous life. There isn't a right answer for what a brave life looks like. Just as God made you unique, your call to courage is unique as well. But believe me, it is a call. You are called to be brave. You are called to face whatever dragons come into your life and scale the mountains that show up in your view. It may be a literal mountain, a mountain of homework, or a mountain of decisions, but it is your journey to walk. And you must walk it bravely. (I wrote a book about it, by the way, if you want to go deeper into what it means to be brave.[1])

But I think we were made for it. Every act of obedience is an act of courage. Every hard yes, every difficult no, every moment of moving and shaking takes bravery. I've felt it in my life, way down deep in my bones, and I've seen it in a hundred lives around me. If you don't believe me, look at the women around you. Find a woman you love and ask her. She'll tell you.

To me these two things go hand in hand. One needs the other. You have to be brave to believe you are made on purpose—to go after your passions and walk in who you were made to be. When you believe God made you on purpose, you are willing to be brave because the root questions are already answered.

Am I enough? Yes, God made you on purpose.

Am I alone? No, God never leaves you. The Bible says He loves everything He makes, and He loves you unconditionally, so you are never alone.

If I mess up, if I fail, if things don't go well, am I done? No, you are always loved, you are never alone, you are enough. So be brave, try the thing, trust that if you are pursuing God and going after a brave life, He can fix and sweep up and help you.[2]

I've tried to make these truths real to me. They are not simple, but the level of difficulty comes in waves. Driving to sit in Jennifer's office for the first time made me face these statements and ask myself how much I believed them. I was saying these things to audiences, talking about them with my friends, and writing them in books, but was I living them? If I'm supposed to be like this, if this is who I really am, why did I still hate me sometimes? If God made me on purpose, what's with all the broken crazy?

And was I really willing to be brave and tell this woman counselor all the things that trouble me? Like, ALL of them? The stuff strangers knew from Twitter, the stuff friends knew from real-life conversations, the stuff no one knew but someone needed to?

Maybe that's where healing comes from, I thought. Maybe being brave about my brokenness was going to bring healing. I would look for it and hope that it was coming along.

Our first meeting went a little like this:

Her: "Hi Annie. Tell me about yourself."

Me: "Oh, hello, everything is fine. My family is perfect. I am practically perfect. No one has ever hurt me; I haven't hurt other people. I'm sure I don't need to be here about anything except this one little sliver of my life—my broken crazy. It's no one else's fault—just my fault—and if you could fix me so I don't kill this relationship with Matt, I would really appreciate it." Ramble ramble ramble—I'm fine—ramble ramble.

And then I sat there and waited for the prescription, the short list of to-dos that would heal me and make me right again. *One and done*, I thought. Ten minutes of intros, half an hour of me explaining the broken crazy, twenty minutes of her fixing me, and we'd be good to go, an hour well spent.

I thought I needed to be repaired. But my need was significantly deeper than that, and that's pretty much the first thing she told me. I actually needed to be rebuilt. And rebuilding anything that is over thirty years old takes a lot of time and strength and perseverance. (I know it's hard for you to imagine life after thirty, but it will be here sooner than you think. What I truly hope is that my story will help you get there with a few less bumps along the way.)

For me, the damage was already done. All the nuts and bolts of my old ways of thinking were rusted in place, and what the broken crazy had done was reveal that the rust was eroding away at my soul, and it was time to tear down the old and build up the new.

I think that's what Paul must have been talking about in his second letter to the Corinthians.

Therefore, if anyone is in Christ, he is a new creation; the old has passed away, and see, the new has come! —*2 Corinthians 5:17*

Now we look inside, and what we see is that anyone united with the Messiah gets a fresh start, is created new. The old life is gone; a new life burgeons!—*2 Corinthians 5:17* MSG

A fresh start. A new creation. Yes and amen. I needed both of those things. But I also needed the strength of heart to hold on until God could complete the work He had begun.

So I have good news for you, dear friend. At this point in your life, you probably don't need to be rebuilt. I'm not saying you don't have some broken parts. I'm just saying you have a few years behind you and lots of years ahead.

I'm gonna guess and say if you're of the female population and have access to a TV or the Internet, you may have seen at least one show on HGTV. Am I right? Just in case, let me now tell you the basic plot of every single episode of every single show. People need houses to live in, and they want to find just the right one. Sometimes those houses need a lot of work, and sometimes they need to be completely rebuilt. But sometimes they're what is called in the real-estate business "move-in ready." This means the guts of the house are good. The foundation is sturdy, there's a fresh coat of paint on the walls, and all the house needs is the people and their stuff.

This is how I see your life today. You're not a fixer-upper. You don't need to be flipped. You're move-in ready. You've (hopefully) got your foundation in place—Jesus. You've even put some fresh paint on the walls. Maybe you're reading your Bible pretty regularly like I was in high school and college. You're going to Bible studies, building relationships with other young women who love the Lord. The house is ready for you to fill up with stuff and make it your own. If you were moving in to your first house, what are the things you would most want to fill it with? That painting you made your freshmen year of high school? That funky cookie jar you got as a white elephant gift last year? Your grandmother's china? It's up to you. You get to fill the house and make it yours.

And you get to fill this life you've been given. What passions has God put in you? What makes you smile? What makes you feel free? That's how you build a life of lovely.

When I was in college, over a decade ago, I went to counseling for a semester. Are you sensing a theme in my life? SISTER NEEDS PROFESSIONAL HELP AT TIMES. (And by the way, there's no shame in going to someone who can help you sort out the stuff that feels out of place in your life. You're not weak if you feel like you can't do this on your own. Wanting to put broken things back in place is not a bad thing—it's absolutely the right thing. And keeping those things in the right places is just plain smart.)

One day in my appointment, we began to dig into some of my old habits, old ways, and the lies I so fully embraced: God didn't love me as I was. I was never enough for Him. I would always be a second-class citizen of the kingdom of God because I wasn't pretty enough and sinned too much. To stick with the rusty metaphor, this may have been the first sign that something was out of sorts and needed to be repaired. Had we caught it there, had I held on for God to complete the work, this most recent rebuilding may not have been so severe.

I left one particular appointment in absolute shambles. I don't know why the counselor let my little twenty-year-old self walk out of the office in that emotional state just because the timer dinged, but we had dug deep and then left the wound absolutely gaping. I went home to my two-bedroom apartment, still crying, and my roommate wasn't home. Just a few doors down lived two of our best guy friends, so I went over there. Tate was sitting on the couch, watching television. I sat down beside him, crossed my legs, leaned onto his shoulder, and cried for an hour.

"You okay?" I remember him asking. "Do you need to talk about anything?" I think that was his gentle way of saying, "UHMMM, WHAT IS GOING ON? THIS IS FREAKING ME OUT."

I said I was fine, I just needed to sit there, and he let me.

I never went to another appointment with that counselor. I quit. Right there. I cried the night away, and then I walked away from the journey. I didn't let God finish what He started. I didn't stay on the operating table. I got up and walked away because all I saw was pain and hurt, no beauty.

I felt some of those same pressures and same desires those first few weeks of counseling with Jennifer. Once the Matt situation started to work itself out a bit, and I felt like we were talking through the fears I had, I was ready to stop . . . you know, right before it actually got personal and in my space.

I had walked away from this place before when I was a junior in college, but now I was more broken and wounded and knew that to dig into it would be, well, more. I decided that if I was really going to survive this, it had to be worth it. It had to have some sort of worthy redemption. It had to be beautiful.

I can't say exactly why, but I decided to stick it out this time, to really try to see if there was a healthier version of me that was just on the other side of the broken crazy. There wasn't a beautiful window view like at Trisha's office, but I could feel something beautiful growing in me. Very small, seed-like, but I saw it there. Jennifer and I discussed, at length, what it was going to take for me to stay in the process, to let it work itself out, to not give up.

It was going to take a lot of finding the lovely in my life. I needed to find a reason to show up and not give up on this critical step in my journey. As I thought back over my own life, the beautiful things, though sometimes spaced uncomfortably far apart, were the knots on the rope that helped me keep climbing. In Trisha's office, it was the view out the window. With Jennifer, and the broken crazy, it was the hope that there was something more beautiful just outside my own view.

There is a correlation, I'm finding, between beauty and perseverance. It feels like beauty might be knots in the rope you are climbing, gas stations along the cross-country journey, the water stations strategically set up on a racecourse. Beauty is what makes it possible to keep going. And beauty is in the eye of the beholder, isn't it? It's not just in the things everyone sees, but it is what YOU see, what sticks out to you, the unique moments God gives you to collect and hold onto and draw strength from.

Had I seen the beauty in finishing a drill with the soccer team, celebrating the strength of suffering together, I wouldn't have pulled up limp.

Had I seen any beauty in me, maybe I wouldn't have walked such an unhealthy path for so long.

I needed to find beautiful if I was going to hang in there. I need it in my life. I need it in my heart. I need it in the bank of my soul to withdraw from when things feel hard. So I decided to start looking.

I have spent significant time over the last few years looking for these moments and building this life of lovely, actively pursuing it, trying to find it around every corner, and ever hoping it is just right there because I do love beautiful things. But mostly I just don't want to quit anymore. I pulled out old photo albums of trips and memories, and I opened my eyes wider (if possible—I already have froggy-wide eyes) to the world around me.

So I'm digging deep and building a life of lovely. And I want you to do the same. I'm filling my mind and eyes and memories with good things, good gifts from God, so that my tank is refueled, so that my parched throat is soothed, before the journey continues.

And I usually start looking around 7:00 a.m.

-Section 2-

Collecting Lovely

Sunrise

Hallelujah!
You who serve God, praise God!
Just to speak his name is praise!
Just to remember God is a blessing—
now and tomorrow and always.
From east to west, from dawn to dusk,
keep lifting all your praises to God!

—PSALM 113:1–3 MSG

 I am a morning person. I know, I know. It's almost embarrassing to admit because it sounds like such a grown-up truth, and I try to avoid saying too many adult-ish things. So take me or leave me, but if you take me, you're taking a person who starts to smile and talk about four seconds after her eyes are open.

Also I don't drink caffeine. I used to, and I used to drag around for the first two hours of my morning until caffeine was pumping through my veins. But it's been about seven years since I quit caffeine, and it changed me into a morning person. The annoying kind.

I don't know what your mornings look like, but my mornings start around 7:00 a.m. So I'm no "four o'clock in the morning I'm at the gym if you need me and I've already read my entire Bible" kind of morning person. I like to wake up with the sun, not before it.

One of the windows in my bedroom faces east. When I'm lying in bed, my feet point to the window so I can see directly out. Every night one of my last ritual behaviors (I have about seventeen we can talk about someday) is to open the plantation blinds of that one window. Because that means the next morning, whenever the sun decides to rise, I will too. I set my alarm a little before 7:00 a.m., or a little after, but I rarely need it. The brightness of the first yellowish-white rays will bore into my eyelids, and no amount of tossing and turning will block the warmth, so I'm up. (Now realistically I may still choose to toss and turn and bask in the warmth, but I'm awake. Which is the goal.)

Don't get me wrong; with the right circumstances in place, I can sleep late with the best of them. Give me a blackout curtain, and I can accidentally rise about the same time I'm supposed to be making lunch. But if that became a habit, I'd miss my favorite time of day.

I've long been a fan of sunrises. (If you're not familiar with this phenomenon, it is the opposite of the sunset and happens first thing in the morning.) Whether seeing one over the wing of a plane or from the crest of a hill out in the country or sitting on the beach, there's something calming and beautiful about the sunrise. It's always going to happen, but it is never the same twice.

I know all this sounds awfully serene, but I realize your sunrise hour may look a little different from mine. Maybe you have an early class and mornings are rushed. Maybe you're running out the door in your gym clothes to get a few minutes in on the treadmill before jogging to class with a bagel in hand.

At my house, that 7:00 a.m. hour has sacredness to it. Kidless, manless, it is quiet and still, and nothing wants to move except the morning sun. I can sit on my brown leather couch and just watch out the window as the sun that woke me continues to rise over the church that sits across the street from my home. The normalness of the view is calming for me, and the sun, doing a version of what it does every day, tells my soul that it will happen again tomorrow, just as it did yesterday.

Sometimes I need a reminder that tomorrow is going to come. That simple. No big flashy thing, just a simple reminder that I will make it through to the sunset and, whatever the night holds, tomorrow morning will come. When my heart is broken or when the night seems long or when the darkness feels consuming, please God promise me tomorrow comes in hues of soothing orange and fiery red and a pink that speaks of kindness. His mercies are new every morning, right? That's what the Bible says in Lamentations 3:22–23, and I believe it. I believe it when I read it on the page, but I see it in a sunrise. Today is as brand-new to God as it is to me.

I find distinct beauty in the everyday sunrise, the normalcy of it. When the sun hits a certain point in the sky, I don't even have to look at a clock because I know it's 8:00 a.m. and it's time to get moving. And I thank God for those mornings that feel regular. And I thank Him for the ones that feel like art.

I speak each summer at the Bloom Conference in Hawaii. (I know, my life is full of sacrifice and hardship.) But included in the realm of things that actually are kind of hard, there is a six-hour time difference between Honolulu and Nashville. So my first few nights there, when my friends want to eat dinner at 8:00 p.m., my body thinks it is 2:00 a.m., and I can barely keep my eyes open to order from the menu.

The upside? I am bright-eyed and bushy-tailed at about 4:00 a.m. Long before the sun sees the beach, I've changed out of my pajamas and put on my workout clothes—almost always a gray T-shirt, black capri leggings, and my mint-and-gray Nikes—and I'm quietly sneaking out the back door and making my way to the ocean. The beach is about a five-minute walk, so I head to the path when the sun is just releasing its first shades. I try to get to this one piece of driftwood in time for the show to start. The log has been there for three years now and has probably played host to many sitters throughout the days and the years. But a few mornings a year, I sit there to watch the sun rise, to literally watch our globe spin, to watch the night become day.

It's unfair to attempt to describe the sight to you, but I'm gonna go for it. The sky starts a dark blue; the ocean looks black.

The stars have retired, but the expanse is early-morning dark. The sky in front of me changes first, lightening in blues until some pinks appear right along the horizon. The top of the sun, on the back side of the ocean, peeks over the water, and the sliver is so small and so bright it looks like a branding iron just out of the fire. It reflects off the water, and as a few minutes pass, the branding iron doubles in size. The sky responds to the fire colors in a subtle way at first, spreading across my whole view. I work so hard to strike the balance between watching it and taking pictures for Instagram and trying to memorize every second so I can keep it forever. I want to eat it. I want to hold it. I want to freeze it in time, every time. Because it's not just the reds and yellows and sunrise shades; it's the aqua greens of the water and the blues of the sky above my head and the whites of the clouds. I see hues at play that don't have names and can't be described. And the sun slowly shows more and more of its morning redness, and the ocean mirrors it, and the sky mirrors it, and it seems like I can see fifty different colors, and within minutes my entire view is an explosion. It lasts for three to four minutes, and then the sun is up, the sky is blue, the clouds are white, and the day has begun.

God orchestrates it. I know He does. Something like that doesn't happen without a Conductor. And yet it can't be timed, and it is not a predictable show. It is an incredible artistic gesture by God for lots of people, but it often feels just for me.

I love when the darkness ends, don't you? Maybe that's the whole thing. Maybe I find so much breathtaking beauty in the sunrise not so much because of what is starting but more because of what it signals has ended. And the darkness *always* ends.

LOOK FOR LOVELY

Here's our chance to make this real. I don't want you to just read about my experiences and how I find those moments of lovely in my own life. I want you to do it. I want you to look around, collect those moments, and start to craft a life of lovely. So let's get started.

First task—set your alarm tomorrow to see the sunrise. Don't tell me you don't know when it happens because one Google search will tell you the exact minute. (Oh, technology, we love you.) About twenty minutes before the sun is to rise, get in a place where you can see the eastern sky. That way you see how dark it is before dawn. You know it in your heart. If your life feels so dark that sometimes you have no idea where the light is going to come from, go there early and watch the sunrise.

And afterward? Read Psalm 19. You'll thank me later.

Tragedy

"Come to me, all you who are weary and burdened, and I will give you rest. Take my yoke upon you and learn from me, for I am gentle and humble in heart, and you will find rest for your souls. For my yoke is easy and my burden is light."

—MATTHEW 11:28-30 NIV

 When my mom's first text of the day is, "Are you awake?" I always worry. It means she needs to call, and it means something is wrong.

Always.

And today started that way. I was awake. So she called to tell me a lifelong friend had been in a car wreck, and his wife, a friend of mine from college, was killed. It sucked the breath right out of my lungs. Deep sadness interrupted my Friday morning. And as I leaned on my dresser in disbelief, about to dry my hair, another friend sent a text about her family emotionally

65

imploding the night before. Heartbroken, she had locked herself in the basement and didn't want to come out. And yes. She is the mom.

I sat down on the chair in my room, wide-eyed. I could have driven across town to be with her, but since I did not have a key to her basement, that would not be totally helpful. I could do nothing to help her or my friend who had just lost his wife.

My phone buzzed. An update about an emergency appendectomy that happened two days before. GOOD GRAVY. IT WAS NOT EVEN EIGHT O'CLOCK IN THE MORNING YET.

It was too much.

Where is the beauty in any of this? How am I supposed to tell you to look for and find beauty when tractor trailers run amuck and kill people you love? When conversations turn to fights turn to yelling matches turn to silence and separation? When surgeries are sudden and painful and expensive?

Just last week I heard a story of a friend's broken heart over a relationship that didn't work. My mind goes back there. When he explained it, he said, "This is the most profound pain of my life. But it also feels sacred." You know me, I was telling him to ask God to HEAL HIM NOW and LET THE PAIN END, and he's sitting there, shattered, saying, "No. I need this. I need to know God here. It feels important."

Sacred.

I don't think like that in sadness. I think about how I want to lay my head on my desk and cry, how I want Jesus to come back right now and make it all right. It doesn't feel sacred; it feels unfair. In every situation. We wake up and hear about yet another school shooting, and we feel numb. We can't process this kind of pain and evil. We see images of floods and fires and children separated from their parents, and it's too much. It all feels wrong, and we just want to shut down.

I want it all to end. I want the betrayals to end and the deaths to stop and the pain to leave. I don't want to persevere through this or learn something new or find beautiful.

I just want to be sad.

So I turn to Ecclesiastes 3, looking for some sort of balm to heal my soul, or at least quiet the burn. And the heading of the chapter is "The Mystery of Time."

Yes, mystery.

There is an occasion for everything,
and a time for every activity under heaven:
a time to give birth and a time to die;
a time to plant and a time to uproot;
a time to kill and a time to heal;
a time to tear down and a time to build;
a time to weep and a time to laugh;
a time to mourn and a time to dance;
a time to throw stones and a time to gather stones;
a time to embrace and a time to avoid embracing;

a time to search and a time to count as lost;
a time to keep and a time to throw away;
a time to tear and a time to sew;
a time to be silent and a time to speak;
a time to love and a time to hate;
a time for war and a time for peace.
—*Ecclesiastes 3:1–8*

God gives us permission to feel. We don't have to numb the pain. There's no demand on your life to bite the bullet and be stronger than the hurt. Yet the directive is the same: rejoice in your sufferings, persevere in them, let your character grow, and watch as hope blooms.

But ugh. I don't feel that today. I feel the suffering. I can't see into the future enough to see what hope is going to look like in any of these situations, but I do know that I'm being given the chance to stand at the starting line again, to start back at Romans 5:3 and stay on this path until Romans 5:5 is living and active in me again. We don't ever get to go back and do things over again. Wouldn't that be great if we could? What we get to do is keep moving forward from pain to perseverance and all the way on to hope.

I'm not sure I'll find beautiful in this. But the only way to truly see beauty, for my heart to grow in capacity and in ability to love and cherish, is through pain and heartache.

In the most simple and not profound way, I think about when I got my ears pierced in middle school. It hurt like whoa, but I finally fit in with all my friends and quickly bought a pair of tiny silver dolphins to wear. I also, soon after that, purchased a pair of earrings where the front was a pig's face and the back was the pig's legs, so it looked like each pig on each ear had stuck it's head through my earring hole and it's body still hadn't come through. So that should give you some idea of my fashionista ways of eighth grade.

I had a friend who, early in high school, decided to turn his pierced ears into gauges. You know, when people stretch the hole in their ears from simply holding an earring to holding wooden dowels of different sizes. I've never done it, but I have heard that it hurts like crazy each time you upgrade to the next size gauge. But it's for a purpose. The only way you can fully experience the next level is by experiencing some pain.

Clearly this doesn't compare to the actual tragedy of losing a spouse or family arguments, but I think of it because I remember that there are times in our lives when we choose to experience physical pain in order to increase our joy.

It's what happens on the volleyball team or the soccer team or the cheerleading squad, isn't it? You want to make varsity, so you put in the work to get where you want. You push through the pain and the hard for the reward that comes with making the team or winning a championship game. It's what happens when you want to be valedictorian or get on the dean's list. You make sacrifices, you study hard, you make choices with your time that aren't always easy or popular. You are willing to feel the pain for the greater good on the other side.

I look at my own story, at the tragedy that happened in my life, and my heart, at nine years old, when I stopped being Annie and started trying to fix Annie and make her right again. For years after that I worked hard to cover my feelings, to eat enough that it stuffed down the pain, to escape hurt at any cost.

I can see that as a thread throughout my story. I don't want to feel pain or sadness. I want to avoid it.

I have an adult onset allergy to dairy. In my former life as an eat-whatever-you-want type gal, ice cream, yogurt, cheese, and milk were normal staples in my everyday. So those types of foods were central to my stuffing down of feelings and smothering of pain. Just as milk is used to calm the heat of spicy food, I used it just the same—to soothe and coat and cover all that was painful.

And then in 2013, I couldn't do that anymore. When I ate dairy, my face and chest and hairline and head and neck would break out into a rash and begin to itch under my skin. I had to cut it out of my eating habits.

Just like that, instead of eating ice cream until my pain subsided or disappeared, I had to look at my pain. And feel it. I had to sit in the uncomfortable and unfamiliar areas of hurt and figure out what to do with the actual feelings and the experiences. And when the broken crazy got loud that summer, I just couldn't stuff it down.

No more smothering. No more pain avoidance. No more ice cream.

Those first days of walking away from dairy, the first days I really started to take my health seriously and listen to what my body wanted, so much pain bubbled up and bubbled over. So much trauma from my childhood and adolescence began to surface when it was no longer sedated. And I had no choice but to feel it all—the hurt from what others said to me, the pain of carrying secrets, and the worry and anxiety that riddled my mind. I didn't know how to talk about it. Though it had been years since the things happened, I really only started to feel them when I quit drowning my sorrows in milk.

It probably hasn't been years since your pain. In fact, maybe you're right smack in the middle of it. If you are, that's okay. You don't have to push it aside. It's okay to feel pain.

Maybe you haven't felt this kind of pain yet that I'm describing. I'm sorry to say it will come. Sometimes in little, rolling waves that feel manageable. You'll be able to see over the next one, and you'll know that after a while they will smooth out on their own. But sometimes it will come in blinding, stinging crashes with no end in sight. Either way, you don't have to drown in your pain. Because always, always on the other side, there is beauty.

Over the past three years, my experience of pain and hurt has deepened. One of the hard parts of writing books is that not everyone in your life gives you permission to tell the stories you live, so to honor others, there are some stories I cannot tell. But within the last few years, I have experienced depths of heartbreak that I truly did not know were possible. I have never felt more alone, more abandoned, more misunderstood. While I was digging through old pains and problems, the world did not stop, and sin did not let up, and so for six or so months, I was pelted from the inside and the outside with more pain than I had previously known.

And I survived. I didn't quit. I didn't walk away from the pain or give up on life. I walked all the way through it, holding the hands of many trusted friends and my counselor, and here I am on the other side. My counselor was right; my capacity to see beauty has increased in a much bigger measure than the pain I felt. My ability to feel the depths of something good was strengthened by my choice to feel the depths of pain. I don't exactly know how it works. I just know the more I hang on and feel, the more I am able to feel; and each time more balm gets rubbed into the wounds of my soul.

It's sacred, right? Feeling God right here, in the middle, is just as my friend described. Purely sacred.

So crafting this life of lovely is not some sort of cheerleader chant. I'm not waving pom-poms at you, trying to convince you that things shouldn't hurt if you are "doing this right." In fact, I'd say it's the other way around. It's not about pretending everything is beautiful and nothing is ugly and you have no questions or doubts and picking out the beautiful in your everyday is going to protect you from anything hurting ever. It's about feeling the pain, letting the sufferings be a part of your life, embracing the Romans 5:3 moments so you can process through the Romans 5:4 days so you live a Romans 5:5 hope-filled life.

I'm sorry if that's not the good news you were looking for. I know it's probably not a popular message today. There are no self-help books telling us how to get our feelings hurt or how to suffer. You know why? Because it happens to all of us. We don't have to look for it. We can't avoid it, so we may as well learn how to make it work for us.

If you aren't experiencing pain, you aren't experiencing beauty. Darkness makes us appreciate the beauty of the light. If you aren't allowing yourself to feel the hurt, sadness, loneliness, and disappointment this fallen world has to offer, you probably aren't feeling the fullness of the joy and beauty the redeemed moments have to offer.

There is nothing beautiful about a tragedy. My friend dying in a freak car accident? Not beautiful. And we feel that. Deeply. The pain of broken relationships and broken hearts sometimes is deeper than words can describe. But there is beauty in choosing to feel that pain, in calling hurt what it is, and not pretending everything is okay.

Whatever tragedy you have experienced or are currently living through, the most beautiful thing you can do is LIVE. Keep walking, keep weeping, keep eating. Don't ignore the hurt. Don't attempt to avoid it and just move on with your life. Feel it all, and invite people in to feel it with you.

LOOK FOR LOVELY

I don't know what you need, friend. But maybe today is the day you pick up your phone and call a person and say how bad it really is. Maybe it's time to call a tragedy a tragedy.

Don't let that nagging voice in your head that says, "They won't understand," keep you from doing what needs to be done. No one can help you unless they know what's going on. We just weren't meant to travel this life alone. Before you pick up the phone, go ahead and say a little prayer. Maybe this is the first time you've even talked to God about your pain. Invite Him in. He's already there, but He longs for us to come to Him when we are worn out. Then ask God for strength to tell someone and for grace for the person who listens. Ask Him to dig down deep in your heart and pull up that pain so you can let others see it.

Seeds

 A few years ago our little neighborhood decided to start hosting its own farmers' market. Every Tuesday from May through October, the field beside the picnic pavilion fills up with local farmers bringing the spoils of their labor.

I've always loved a fresh farmers' market. Maybe it's the romantic in me, and I feel like Kathleen Kelly from *You've Got Mail* when Joe Fox buys a mango as they stroll through the Upper West Side market, or maybe it's because I was the girl who would read lots of novels about the olden days when everyone was a pioneer and working in the fields first thing in the morning. But for me, there is something about shopping at a farmers' market that makes me feel connected to a simpler time.

I grew up going to Burger's Market. It's just down Canton Highway from my parents' house, and the storefront looks the same today as it did when I was a kid. Big red letters spell out BURGER'S MARKET above the doors with a cutout of a red tomato between the two words. Instead of a parking lot in front, there is a nursery full of rows of live plants and flowers. My grandmother used to love to buy hanging plants from Burger's. It was never a quick decision, and I would shuffle and sweat as I stood beside her on the asphalt under the midday sun while she picked between the purple flowers and the light purple flowers.

Inside, in the open-air store, is every type of in-season fruit and vegetable. Mom always sent me to get squash and tomatoes while she got potatoes and onions. In the back are some local Georgia things like peanut brittle and jams. Burger's is wall-to-wall fresh food. And even with all the issues I had with food, I could look around Burger's and think it was awesome. I think that little place deep down in me that longed to be healthy found a little home there in Burger's.

So each week here in Nashville at the 12th South Farmers' Market, my soul connects back to being with my grandmother and mom as each tent from each farm is full of only in-season foods. And as they set up, they turn a field of grass into a horseshoe-shaped market, with booths from across Middle Tennessee on either side of the path. I try to go almost every week, even if it is just to get a carton of strawberries or some sherbet from the lady with the rolling ice cream cart and big umbrella. This will not shock you, but my main motivation for attendance is not the vegetables, but neither is it the sherbet. While I am always glad to see what fresh produce makes it to our neighborhood, I'm more excited to see my neighbors.

Nashville is split up into little villages all over town. And many of my friends call 12th South, our little corner of Music City, home. Or they are like me, claiming to be a 12th South resident when I clearly live in Oak Hill. (I claim 12th South because it's where the cool kids live, and I want to be cool. Okay? Okay.) So every Tuesday the likelihood of running into a friend is high because everyone pops down to the farmers' market in the afternoon.

On a normal summer Tuesday, I drive over to Annie and Dave's house, and she and the kids and I will grab our reusable grocery bags and walk down to Sevier Park. We slowly walk the horseshoe-shaped market, her arms loaded up with vegetables, while I pick out a few that I know I like, but definitely feeling the magnetic pull to the goat cheese guy. HE MAKES PIMENTO GOAT CHEESE. I cannot resist him.

Annie and I tool around for an hour or so, even though you can lap the farmers' market in less than ten minutes, because we stop and talk with friends about every ten feet. Miranda is over at the local ranch booth, getting some fresh meat, so I say hi and ask about her new restaurant venture. Amy and Jon are stocking up on blueberries as I overhear her telling Annie about a recipe she is dying to try with blueberries in lasagna. Amber, Hillary, and Laura are sitting at a picnic table, talking over popsicles, so I sneak over to interrupt. I see Katherine pushing Henry in his stroller, and I yell a hi to them. Heather's three-year-old daughter Annabelle runs by, and I snatch her up for a hug, and we walk toward the Mennonite farm tent.

Under the cool of the shady pop-up tent, they have three long tables covered in red-checkered tablecloths and shaped like an upside down U. The left side has carton after carton of strawberries. There are some radishes poking out of wicker baskets toward the back corner where two tables meet like an L. They have some honey and a few loaves of homemade bread beside their cash registers. Then the right side is just a mass of vegetables. Lettuces, onions, kale, yellow squash, cucumbers, and snap peas. At the front are a few huge watermelons that are mostly green, with a few light yellow spots.

Annabelle and I walk out of the sun and into the shade of the tent, and she begins to point to different vegetables and say their color. And when she does, I tell her the name of the produce. We go through the three tables over and over again, to the point it is awkward for me not to buy something from them, so I grab some kale and strawberries to use in my breakfast smoothies. One of the watermelons is sliced, so she and I both grab a little slice as we walk out and thank the lovely Mennonites.

I pick out the slimy black seeds from her piece before she attempts to digest them. I pick them out of my slice, too, and flick them into the grass, silently apologizing for possibly planting a watermelon vine in the middle of Sevier Park.

We walk back to her mom, Heather, and we chat for a bit. Then as the afternoon turns to kid dinnertime, everyone kind of moseys back to the street where they live (or where they park, as is the case for me).

But I can't get those little seeds out of my mind. The tininess of the seed versus the monster size of that beautiful watermelon we sampled. I see the beauty across the farmers' market in the colors and the textures and the vegetables and how our Earth produces just what we need to be healthy.

But again my mind keeps going back to the watermelon seeds. Something about those slimy little seeds has me tearing up.

Those who sow with tears will reap with songs of joy.
Those who go out weeping, carrying seed to sow, will
return with songs of joy, carrying sheaves with them.
—Psalm 126:5–6 NIV

There is something beautiful in the small seeds. And I need to be reminded of that. When my heart is broken and I am weeping, when tragedy hits and I feel like the tears will never stop, when I feel like I've cried an ocean, the Bible says they are just seeds. Then the seeds are planted, covered in dirt, and persevere through the season of growth. Again there's that perseverance. There's that reminder to not give up. Because somehow I sow tears and reap joy. And the joy will be greater.

I'm a crier; it's one of my go-to emotions. At the doctor's office this morning, I cried. Driving home from a funeral last week, I cried. When he broke up with me in a text, I cried. (And later rolled my eyes.) I have sown my fair share of tears, and to be honest, I cannot imagine how God can take that sadness and multiply it in size and turn it to songs of joy. I just don't see the math in that.

But I do see how it adds up when I look at a watermelon at the farmers' market.

Just like a watermelon's seeds are dwarfed in size by the watermelon itself, I see that my weeping and my tears will be minimal compared with my joy. I will go out with seeds and return with sheaves. I can picture sheaves of wheat thanks to Burger's Market and my local farmers' market. I can feel the texture of those tiny seeds in my hands because I picked them out of Annabelle's slice.

I'm looking at some of the joys I'm experiencing in my work—getting to write, having an office with a beautiful desk built by my friend Blake. I've never done this before, but I'm trying to see this as sheaves. This is the multiplication of the tears I sowed when things didn't go well for me professionally—when I got the repeated noes from publishers, when I've had to part ways with people who worked with me, when someone writes a cruel review of my writing on the Internet. Those tears have always seemed so large, but when I really think about it, the Bible is right. These joys are much greater than the sadness.

And what I'm almost too afraid to think about, if I'm being honest with you, is what this means for the tears I've cried over my singleness. Because . . . THEY HAVE BEEN CRIED AND WILL BE CRIED AGAIN. How can something dwarf the heartache and loneliness I've felt my whole adult life? How can that be? I question if it can, to be honest. That's just the truth of what I feel. I love my life, and I'm so grateful for all I have, but it certainly isn't the kind of joy that makes the tears seem tiny.

But then, slimy watermelon seeds. I have to cling to the truth of what will become of those slimy watermelon seeds. That in their season, they will each become lots of watermelons (though hopefully not in the middle of the farmers' market grass), just as every tear I've sown will grow into something joyful and beautiful, far grander than I ever expected. What God will do with my seeds, when I return with songs of joy, is grow them into something full of color and health and variety and joy and blessings for others—just like the farmers' market.

I'm believing what I cannot see because of what I can see. And that's the kind of moment that matters to me—the kind I hang on to, the kind I call lovely, the kind that sticks to my heart and reminds me over and over again of who our God is and how He works.

LOOK FOR LOVELY

Buy a watermelon, the kind with seeds. And look for yourself.

Look at the tears that have fallen recently. Where do you most need to find joy right now?

Hold one of those seeds in your hand, and think of the thing in your life right now that feels insurmountable. What mountain is it that you just know will be impossible to climb? If you need to cry in this process, go ahead. Those tears are like those tiny watermelon seeds. They will fall in many times and in many places. And in their place, someday, there will be joy. More joy than you can imagine today.

Pushing Pause

You've all been to the stadium and seen the athletes race. Everyone runs; one wins. Run to win. All good athletes train hard. They do it for a gold medal that tarnishes and fades. You're after one that's gold eternally. I don't know about you, but I'm running hard for the finish line. I'm giving it everything I've got. No sloppy living for me! I'm staying alert and in top condition. I'm not going to get caught napping, telling everyone else all about it and then missing out myself.

—1 CORINTHIANS 9:24–27 MSG

 I love sports. For as long as I can remember, watching sports and playing sports have been a part of my story and my family life. Because my dad never had any sons, he would always take me and my sisters with him to watch games.

As an adult now, and someone who has friends with kids, I'm still super impressed that when my dad bought two tickets for an Atlanta Falcons game, he would invite me to use one of them, instead of, you know, one of his friends. I mean, I'm pretty fun to hang out with as an adult, but as an eleven-year-old? Not as much.

Dad once took me and my two sisters to an Atlanta Braves game. I was in middle school, so was Tatum, and Sally was just a little kiddo, probably four or five. Dad bought great seats, just a few rows behind first base. It was July, and we all wore our jean shorts and Atlanta Braves T-shirts. (Maybe not Dad. He only wears khaki shorts and button-up shirts.) We grabbed Cokes on our way to the seats. It was a hot day because JULY and ATLANTA. We knew it was hot going into it, but we had no idea how incredibly hot.

One inning. We lasted one inning. My poor dad bought the tickets and Cokes and drove us forty-five minutes to Fulton County Stadium for us to see three men try to hit the ball in the hot July sun. Then, after about half an hour in the stadium, the weeping and gnashing of teeth, the "PLEASE, DADDY, I AM MELTING," the tears from little Sally as her face turned beet red and the sweat soaked her hair, we left.

That should have been enough to run me off of the love for sports, my dislike for being blistering hot and sweaty, but it didn't.

You didn't ask, but I'm gonna tell you anyway. My favorite sport is soccer. Arsenal is my team of choice in the English Premiere League. A close second, a more lifelong viewing sports fan, is American football. The Atlanta Falcons are my team, even if they tend to break my heart at some point every season. I tried to break up with them in the 2013–2014 season to cheer for the team in Nashville, Tennessee Titans, but I just couldn't do it. My heart is red-and-black, for the Falcons and my beloved Georgia Bulldogs.

Before the 2015–2016 season started, my dad and I got to go to the Atlanta Falcons training camp for a day; and if I wasn't a superfan before that (which I probably was), I certainly am now. I spoke at an event in Atlanta in the spring, and then a sweet girl who works for the team offered for me and someone else to be her guests at training camp at the end of the summer. So when I got to pick a plus-one, it was an easy choice of who was going with me. Obviously, Dad. I could not imagine anything cooler. We got to hear from the coaches and see the players practice and stand right on the sidelines of the field. I don't think I stopped smiling for the rest of the day.

Football really is the sport I have grown up loving. Soccer is the one I played, but football is the one I watched. As a high schooler I was the manager of the football team at Sprayberry High School. Yep, that means I spent every week of football season doing sweaty-boy laundry, cleaning up practice equipment, making sure the water coolers were always full, and then the other managers and I would spend Thursday afternoons taking steel wool to every helmet to shine up the gold before the big game on Friday.

But those guys weren't my friends. Of course, I told myself they were because, hello, I wanted to be cool, but I didn't hang out with them outside of school and the field. I didn't text with them or talk with them on the phone. One player came over to my house one night, but that was just because he had asked me to hold a note from his girlfriend before practice and forgot to get it back from me. So he came over to pick it up. They weren't my people, I didn't listen to them talk about their hearts and minds and motivation. (Do high school boys talk about that stuff to anybody? Possibly.)

But then a group of athletes came into my life in 2011, fifteen years later, and those young men did let me hear what was in their minds and hearts.

I remember seeing them as they walked into the college ministry service at my church in December 2011. Five young men, standing side by side, and they looked like massive soldiers. They were all easily over six feet tall, and they were thick and solid. I didn't want to fight any of them because I knew I would lose.

I guessed they were athletes, based on their Vanderbilt baseball sweatshirts. I guessed they were country, based on the light-wash Wranglers and boots. They introduced themselves: Connor was the tall blonde who looked like a Ken doll, Keenan was the tan one with the chiseled face of a superhero. Joel had a buzz cut and seemed shy; Andrew introduced himself like a politician with the smile of a celebrity; and Will wore khakis, had floppy blonde hair, and a suspicious smile. I loved them immediately in the way you love people you want to hang on to forever.

That baseball season, 2012, I spent a lot of time around the table with these guys as our friendship grew, and I became the surrogate big sister to these five and a handful of other players. I listened as they talked about girls (A LOT), baseball, school, and God. I heard them when they talked about what it was like to be an athlete, on the good days and the bad, and I heard something I had never heard before.

They didn't believe in quitting.

You know me. My brain does not work like that. But across the board, every athlete I spoke to told me the same thing—they do not quit. Even after the worst games for Vanderbilt, which were few and far between, none of my boys walked off the field and never returned. The home run king would strike out every at-bat in a game, but he didn't quit. The pitcher would get taken out after two innings because of his poor throws, but he didn't quit. The second baseman would make an error, but he didn't throw his glove and rip off his jersey and leave the ballpark. When they won the national championship in 2014, they didn't drop the mic and never return to the field because they had won everything they needed to win. The athletes I know do not know how to quit.

I was curious, and it started a new theory in my mind. Whether it is nature or nurture or a combination of both, why was an athletic brain so different from my own?

I texted my friend Tim to see if we could meet for coffee. As a standout football player at Penn State and then in the NFL, playing for multiple teams over his seven-season career (most recently the Tennessee Titans!), he's the most athletic athlete I know. And about two years ago, he was diagnosed with ALS. (ALS affects the parts of your brain that help you control your muscles. It gets worse and worse over time, eating away at your ability to walk and talk, and makes it hard to do even more basic human functions, like breathing.)

I didn't know Tim Shaw personally before he had ALS, but since I've known him, I've watched him fight and get loud about the disease, about his desire to beat it, and what that is going to look like for him. Even as his body changes in response to the disease—his strength deteriorates, his hands struggle to grasp things at times, his legs don't hold up under him with the same reliability they used to—he remains positive and upbeat and yet truthful and realistic.

And to be honest, it doesn't make any sense to me. When do you just give up? It's the kind of question quitters ask, I realize. But it is what came to my mind as I parked my car and hopped out, headed toward Tim waiting for me outside the coffee shop.

We met at Steadfast Coffee, and I made him try an almond milk chai even though he totally didn't like it. I wanted Tim to tell me about quitting. I wanted to understand his perspective, to see how he could have any hope after such a devastating and life-changing diagnosis. We talked about football; we talked about his upbringing. He furrowed his brow in confusion when I talked about being a quitter, like it was a word he barely recognized. I laughed then because my native tongue of quitting is a foreign language to a guy like Tim. I almost had to explain to him what I meant.

"You know," I said, "it's just like when a workout at the gym is too hard and I don't think I can finish, I quit." And in my mind I pictured pull-ups—because seriously, I cannot do them.

"No," he responded, "when the weights in the gym are too heavy to lift, you can stop for that day. You can rest. But you go back the next day. And you try again. You keep trying to lift until you are able to do it."

It's almost like we defined *quitting* differently. And, in a lot of ways, we defined *grace* differently too. One mistake, one broken link in a chain, and I'm out. I'm done. I've failed. I quit. Tim taught me the difference between pausing and quitting.

And then Tim talked about his mind and the battle there. The heavy lifting, if you will, of what goes on in the mind of an athlete whose body knew few limits until a disease began to eat away at his strength.

His speech doesn't slur, but it struggles, so you have to listen closely as Tim works to make his voice and throat muscles do what he wants them to do when he talks. It is heartbreaking and hope-filled at the same time. We talked for about an hour, all about quitting and not quitting and what strength actually looks like.

I had one more thing I wanted to ask him that felt a little off-limits, a little out-of-bounds. But as I've watched his physical abilities change, as he is able to do less for himself, and when I read the stats and what is a possible outcome for Tim, I just wondered . . .

"Tim," I asked hesitantly, "at what point do you quit? When do you give up?"

He just stared at me. "I won't quit, Annie."

And I believed him. He won't quit because athletes don't walk away. I see it in him, the mental toughness to be a finisher, and I see it in my Vandy bros. They recognize the value in taking a moment to pause, to rest, to reevaluate. But they don't give up. I thought athletes were stronger than everyone else, but I'm beginning to think they just get grace better than I do. Grace to grow, grace to make mistakes and recover, grace to try again.

I want to be like Tim. I want to erase *quitting* from my dictionary of life and add a little more grace. I want to know that when life eats away at me to the point it feels like I forget how to breathe, that it's okay to push pause. It's okay to rest and regroup. Taking a break isn't the same as quitting.

But there is no way to tie a neat bow on the end of this for Tim. He doesn't know how his body will continue to respond and what his physical strength will be day to day. But he still volunteers at church as a greeter, still smiles when he sees me, still asks if I'm ever going to finish writing this chapter about him.

He's not quitting. He's not giving up. He's full of grace toward himself and others. He has taught me that to pause is to win and to rest can actually be a part of the victory. Tim is winning, I'm proud to be his friend. (And yes, Tim, I finally finished writing about you. Hope you like it. And you really need to give almond milk chai another chance.)

LOOK FOR LOVELY

Maybe the best thing you can do today is pause. Maybe you need a break from something, a little rest. You've been studying days on end for that mid-term, and your brain can't possibly hold another factoid—maybe take a thirty-minute walk and get some fresh air? You've been working late nights and pinching pennies to scrape together enough money for that trip with friends this summer or the mission trip with your church—maybe take some time to relax and do something you enjoy? Crank up your favorite tunes, snuggle up with a fuzzy blanket and a good book—and not one that is required reading!

Don't worry—the project, the exam, the job—everything will still be there tomorrow. You'll pick right back up where you left off. Remember the mind of an athlete teaches us that to keep from quitting, you have to pause.

The Sound of Music

*Cast all your anxiety on him
because he cares for you.*

—1 PETER 5:7 NIV

 I have always loved music. I was in choir for my entire childhood and teen life, the highlight being when I played Little Psalty in our church's children's musical. Psalty was a singing hymnal that taught children about God, and in one particular scene we met the young version of him.

Yes. Little Psalty is a boy. But I would not let my art be confined by gender roles! I slapped that baseball cap on my head and swung the bat over my shoulder and—wearing a cardboard box painted like a hymnal, held on to my body with suspenders—I walked up on stage. There I belted out a few lines of the old hymn "Take My Life and Let It Be." The crowd roared in applause, as much as two hundred parents can roar. But it was, and remains, an absolute highlight of third grade.

I used a hymnal given to me that year by my church choir director, Kibbie DeJarnett, to teach myself to play piano. I knew how to read music enough to read the treble clef line, and I had a beginner's piano book to learn the notes on the keyboard. I would spend hours in my room, with my tiny three-octave keyboard, playing my favorite hymns from church.

But even before that, I remember wearing my ballet tutu at my grandparents' house and dancing around to Burl Ives singing "Lavender Blue."

Probably like you, I can connect just about any year of my life to a song or a musical experience that has been a part of me.

Ben Rector's album *Into the Morning* was in my earbuds through the subways and cab rides of my first full-week visit to New York City.

I will always think of the Vineyard Music album called *If You Say Go* when I think of my senior year of college. I made all the big decisions with those songs in my head.

Matt Wertz sang "Capitol City" my whole drive to Nashville, when I decided to move.

As I drove to teach elementary school every morning for five school years, I sang "Legacy" by Nichole Nordeman as a prayer over my students.

Can you do that too? Link songs or albums or musical experiences to particular seasons of your life?

My high school did musicals, and since I had joined the chorus instead of continuing to play the French horn after middle school (one of my few life regrets because how cool would I be right now if I could play the French horn?), I got to be in the *Sound of Music*, which was amazing. It didn't put in me a longing to chase a Broadway dream to 42nd Street in New York, but I absolutely loved the experience, the darkness of the room and the music soaring through the crowd.

I went to see a few musicals (done by professionals, not the Sprayberry High School chorus) as I was growing up, but it wasn't until college that I had a breathtaking experience around the sounds and the sights and the feel of musical theater.

Some friends had told me about *Les Misérables*, and I had seen the music performed on a PBS special on television, so I knew a lot of the words. I watched that special any time it came on, and in fact, I had recorded it so I could watch it whenever it came to mind. The musical was being performed at the Fox Theater, a beautiful theater in the heart of downtown Atlanta. Ten or so of us bought tickets together—the cheapest seats we could find, sitting in the back row of the balcony—and we drove the ninety miles from the University of Georgia for it.

I didn't know the whole story, just the songs. And as I watched, and the revolt broke out on stage, and characters died heartbreaking deaths, and those scenes mixed with those beautiful songs and lyrics, tears came to my eyes. I don't remember experiencing music that big before—the voices, the large orchestra. All of it almost overwhelmed my senses and left my jaw ajar that such a beautiful experience was wrapped in song.

I saw the power of music that night in a way I had never seen outside of church.

Now I'm addicted to musicals. If they are playing in Nashville, I want to attend. But when I'm in New York City, it is absolutely a must-do. In fact, just last week, my dear friend Jonathan and I went to see *Finding Neverland* on Broadway. It is a movie I have long loved because I love Johnny Depp and I love Peter Pan, and so the movie was an instant classic for me. As soon as I heard of the musical and that Matthew Morrison, Broadway star and Mr. Schuester on the television show *Glee*, would be starring in it, I texted Jonathan. He lives in New York, so I often tend to send him, "NEXT TIME I AM IN NEW YORK WE MUST..." texts. I had done that with this musical, that we MUST see it together next time I was in New York. And being the faithful friend he is, he turned down other offers and waited until I arrived in New York City to see it.

We bought matinee tickets the morning of the show, and lucked out getting tickets toward the center just about ten rows back. We had full view of the stage, and I smiled from ear to ear the moment we sat down. The lights dimmed and the curtain parted, and I was in awe for the next two hours. The music was beautiful, the performances were incredibly strong, and I won't ruin the ending for you, but I will expose Jonathan and say that we were both WEEPY for the last half hour of the show. It was just unreal. And moving. And I wanted to see it again the next day. Or at least sit in the dark theater with my eyes closed and listen to it all over again.

What is it about music that does that to us? There's something about a song that can take us back to a place, to a memory. But I also think music heals something in us—it soothes, it blesses, it covers. I think our brains and our bodies know how to collect moments like that. According to an article in *Psychology Today*, there is a lot of science behind the connection between sounds and memories.[3] I feel that in me, and I feel what happens when music binds up something that feels like it has fallen to pieces inside of me.

Maybe that's why David wrote so many psalms. Maybe for him, just like for me with Psalty songs, there's a connection that he craved as an adult, and he found it in the sounds of his childhood. The songs he sang as a shepherd boy, maybe those are the same ones that rang through the castle when he was king. Because there is comfort there, don't you agree?

As God built perseverance in me and cleaned my soul of the broken crazy, my days were particularly marked by a few albums on repeat in my head and heart. For a while, it was all Bethel Music's *We Will Not Be Shaken*. The third track, "Jesus We Love You," became my airplane song, the one I would play anytime we were high above the clouds. Then it switched to Hillsong United's *Empires*. My life season switched as well; I went from being in a place where I felt like God was advancing things to a season of waiting and watching and trusting and wondering. And that album held me through it.

I think something shifts in my head and heart and atmosphere when worship is playing. Most mornings when I'm getting ready, I will play whatever album I'm addicted to currently—right now it's Steffany Gretzinger's *Blackout*—and let the music play through my Apple TV so that it fills the house. My day starts differently when it starts like that.

You may laugh at me, but I clearly remember the first worship music I ever bought. Until I was in high school, I didn't know that you could own the songs we listened to in church. I mean, we obviously had kid Christian music like Psalty, but I didn't have any grown-up stuff until my senior year of high school. At a winter retreat called In the Vine, the worship band sold their CDs outside the meeting room. I bought one for $5 and immediately went back to my bunk to listen to it. For the entire free time, three hours, I lay on the top bunk by the window and listened to that five-song CD over and over again, amazed that I could actually own it myself. The songs that moved me to tears in the worship center were now in my ears.

I know, that's almost laughable now when we can hear a song online and own it on our iPhone in less than a minute, but in high school? It blew my mind. And it changed my life. I filled my home life and car life with worship music after that retreat. It was the sea I swam through.

The summer after my sophomore year of college, I was a youth group intern, but about three weeks in, the youth pastor left and took a full-time pastoring job. Suddenly this fun part-time job with a youth pastor I loved being around became my full-time, full-stress lonely job. The students, parents, and church were awesome. It was just that I was twenty. I had no idea how to run an entire youth group—to meet all their spiritual needs as well as their fun youth group summer hangout needs. But sometimes it's those moments you get thrown into that you absolutely ARE NOT READY FOR that build the most character in you.

I worked really hard. And I went home every night and practically melted down. The stress to please and to create and to organize was more than I felt I could handle.

So every night around 10:00 p.m., I would watch *Mary Poppins.*

Yep. The whole thing. I usually fell asleep with twenty or so minutes left, but every night I watched it. There was something about the simplicity of the story and the connection to my childhood and the music. It all combined to be the force that kept me getting up and going back to work the next day.

I would cry, often, when Julie Andrews sang "Stay Awake" to help the Banks children fall asleep. It felt like she was taking care of me, protecting me, wishing me well. I know that sounds kind of ludicrous, but it was what worked and was balm for my soul. It was the moment I collected; it was the lovely I found in a life where stress was thrown at me suddenly. And the music would reverberate through my mind all day long.

As I said, I have always loved music. But I wouldn't categorize myself as a musically talented person, though I wish I were. (I sing like I think I'm a great singer.) I've had musical moments through the years, like when I taught myself to play the piano as a kid or learned French horn in middle school. I even learned to play the guitar in college because I was a Christian in college, and that kind of feels like a spiritual rite of passage, know what I mean? But I'm not stellar in any of the instruments. I live in a town full of people who play instruments for a living, who feel about music the way I feel about words on pages, who have found a calling and a ministry in song. That's not me, but I'm thankful those people exist because they are the ones who make the music that moves me. I'm not the kind who listens for certain chords and notes and such, but when a song resonates with me, I don't forget it.

Just this week, I was FaceTiming with my friends Matthew and Brittany as they were putting their children to bed. The last thing they do is sing together and pray; and as we were all sitting there, their oldest, Parker, started to sing . . .

"I caaaast all my caaaares upon Youuuuu, I laaaaay all of my burdens down at Your feet. And anytiiiime I don't knoooow, wha-at to do, I will caaaaast all my caaaares upon Youuu."[4]

And as I listened to her, my mind took me back to the bedroom of my childhood, memories flooded of learning to play the piano and singing along to every Psalty record. I was reminded that I knew that song in a time when I worried a lot. Constantly. And when I couldn't fall asleep, or when I woke up and felt panic or sick to my stomach, that's the song I would sing. I started to sing along with her, thinking of my day and my own worries and what was going on in my life; and after we hung up, I was still singing. And praying. And remembering all the times God really did take my cares upon Himself and let me rest.

That's what music does. It holds you together when you think you'll fall apart. It reminds you of truth. It grabs your hand as you try to cross the finish line. It fills your ears with peace when it feels like there is no peace.

LOOK FOR LOVELY

Thanks to the gift of technology, we have nearly limitless options for discovering new music and keeping our ears and hearts filled with it every day. If you haven't tuned into anything new lately, I challenge you to find a new worship album to download. And when you buy it, listen all the way through.

If you grew up in church, maybe pick an old worship song you haven't heard in a long time. Put it on repeat, and let it bring back memories of what the Lord was orchestrating in your life during those months or years. Remember. Remember what it felt like the first time you heard the song. Remember why the words stir up so much emotion in you. Remember why you lifted your hands.

Don't know any worship songs? That's okay. Ask your friends or your social media network. Still can't find a good one? I'll help you get started. Check out Steffany Gretzinger!

Nail Polish

Your beauty should not come from
outward adornment, such as elaborate
hairstyles and the wearing of gold jewelry
or fine clothes. Rather, it should be that of
your inner self, the unfading beauty of
a gentle and quiet spirit, which is of great
worth in God's sight.

—1 PETER 3:3–4 NIV

 My hands don't look like kid hands anymore. They don't look bad or weird or ugly; they just don't look young anymore. Getting older is a weird thing. In a Western culture that teaches that beauty is found in youth, the process of slowly seeing that fade away is interesting and different from what I would have predicted.

If nobody has said it to you already, I'll tell you—you don't have to be afraid of getting older. It's weird, yes, but not bad. I think I've managed to embrace this transition mostly with grace and not hide the fact that I am no longer the teen I once was.

Except when it comes to my fingernails. While my hands most assuredly look like the hands of a mid-thirty-year-old woman, my fingernails are painted with all the accoutrements of your average seventeen-year-old gal. No shame here.

I see my hands a lot. It's a part of the job, the fact that I type all day every day. So my hands sit right here, in front of my face. A neon yellow is my current nail polish color of choice. I find the bright colors to be my favorite, even though they can be mildly (or mostly) distracting. Each of my ring fingers is painted with the neon yellow and silver glitter on top. Yes, I am channeling my inner '80s child this week. But I like seeing the brightness and the sparkle dance across my keyboard as I type. It speaks of deeper things to me. An outward sign of a healthy heart.

I have been a nail-biter most of my life. As an elementary-age student, I bit and picked at my nails until they bled. I bit my nails when I was nervous. I bit my nails when I was bored. I bit my nails when I was sad, lonely, busy, scared. It really didn't matter. I bit them down until you could see the tips peeled to deeper levels and the nail bed would be revealed on each finger. It was ugly.

As a teenager I continued the habit. The idea of having pretty nails never crossed my mind. Why would I focus on such tiny details when the big picture felt hopeless? Is changing the light switches in a room really going to do all that much to cover up the hideous wallpaper?

While still living in Georgia, however, I started to join friends at the nail salon more often. As the Lord was healing my mind, I slowly attempted to defeat the habit and try to keep a color of some sort on my hands. Biting my nails was a habit that needed to be broken. Bottles of "stop biting" nail polish piled up in my bathroom drawers. After a bad day, I would revert to biting my nails again and then begin the process all over again. In time the old habit died with the old mind-set, but I still would pick at and mess with my nails when I was having emotional struggles. By the time I moved to Nashville, the paint on the nails was the first to go, versus having my hands in my mouth and biting until they were throbbing with pain.

Now the habit is almost (almost!) defeated. It's a super-rare, super-nervous day that my nails take a hit.

During the broken crazy season of my life, I sat down to breakfast with my friend Sonnie at Star Bagel in Sylvan Park, a quaint and quirky little neighborhood just west of downtown Nashville. We were catching up with life, having not seen each other for a while. As I picked up my breakfast to eat, Sonnie noticed that not only were my nails not painted, but they were tiny, red, and wounded.

"Oh my gosh, Annie, your nails!" she said surprised. "What happened?"

I looked down, having not even realized how they looked. Wow. What an outward reflection of an inward pain. I started to tell her everything, where things felt wrong, where the broken crazy had originated, and what I was trying to do to stand up to it, what it felt like when I failed to do so.

I realized that day that my fingernails had become a gauge of sorts. Painted and manicured, all is well. Bare but shaped well, I'm too busy. Bitten down and gross, we've got a problem.

But now it's even more than just a good indicator of my personal and mental health. I find strength in the beauty. These hands are more than how I make a living. They are a subtle reminder of grace in this journey of perseverance. When I am able to hold on when I want to let go, when words go down on paper, or I'm able to lift more grocery bags than I think—that's when I realize my hands are part of the solution to finding beauty, not part of the problem.

So I take my nail polish situation pretty seriously. Which may sound silly to you, and I'm okay with that. But that's the thing about collecting this life of lovely all around you—what you find beautiful may not be what I find beautiful. The moments you collect that will help you finish the thing you've started may not be moments that matter to me.

Oh the beauty of being humans who are allowed to be creatively different, yes?

So I paint my nails. Depending on my mood and the weather and the season and the event. Sometimes it is the new gel shellac situation that can last for a few weeks, but at the rate I like to change colors, gel is usually reserved for international trips or weddings. I'm about half-and-half getting my nails painted at the salon versus painting them myself at home. My personal nail polish collection has grown significantly as people have gifted me lots of bottles, many of them containing glitter. Which, clearly, is a joy to my heart. So I love laying all the shades out and picking the one that is right for the moment and right for the day. (Yes, sometimes I can change daily. I'm so annoying like that.)

Winter brings shades of chestnut and mocha, a personal favorite color being You Don't Know Jacque from OPI. In autumn I love a good gray or a mauve, like my grandmother used to wear. Spring I prefer the light pinks, light gray with sparkles, or Easter egg colors. And summer? It has become my favorite. Brights. Hot pink. White. Orange. Anything that screams "Beach! Laughter! Tan! Fruit! Outside!"

First Peter 3:3–4 speaks of not focusing too much on your outward appearance. It was a warning, at the time, to the women of Israel to not become like the Egyptian women and spend hours focused on outer beauty. Instead, Peter says, spend time on who you are on the inside.

I haven't always liked these verses. (Am I allowed to say that?) They didn't resonate with me because I thought about all the time I spent in church and all the time I spent trying to be the "right person," but I never felt like I had a gentle spirit, and I continued to hate my body. It's a tough time, middle school and high school. What the world tells you and what God says is true about you are always fighting for your attention. You so desperately want to live the way God wants you to live. And what I've found is a lot of times this means we cover up our insides—our real insides—with an outside cloak that is more acceptable to our watching friends. Or we fill up our God bucket with all the things we think He wants us to *do* for Him instead of looking at who He wants us to *be*.

But what I have learned of late is that when I focused on the inside, the outside changed too. The focus isn't on clocking time with God just for the sake of checking off your daily responsibilities. "Did I pray today? Did I read my Bible? Did I journal? Okay, then I'm good!" I tried that for a long time. I thought that was building my strength. But it wasn't. Don't hear me wrong—time with God is essential. Yes, our strength is found in intimacy with this always caring, always good heavenly Father. But just doing those things for the sake of feeling good about yourself isn't doing anybody any good.

When I am doing the hard work of healing for my soul, when I am letting God dig down into the hurt places and expose them and heal them, my body responds with health as well. But when my inside is neglected and hurting, it shows in my hands and in my eyes. It shows in the sadness that can't be denied when someone looks right at me. I am never quiet (if I'm awake), but my spirit can be quiet. My heart can be at rest. And my painted nails will prove that to you.

What in your life paints the picture of the health of your soul? You know those verses I used to not love? Well, 1 Peter 3:3 tells us what beauty should not consist of but is quickly followed by verse 4 telling us beauty should consist of "what is inside the heart—the imperishable quality of a gentle and quiet spirit." I love how Scripture leaves us with this true beauty that will last forever. It doesn't mean I'm going to stop painting my nails or working out or brushing my hair—all activities that make me feel good about myself and help me see lovely. It just means that I notice those things for what they are, put them in their appropriate spot behind the focus of a healthy soul and spirit, and continue to run toward that health.[5]

This is not just a task for today. The discipline of reordering our insides so they always look more like what God wants them to look like is a lifelong task. As an ever-so-slightly-older-than-you woman, I can testify to this. Those birthdays will keep coming, and our outer appearance will change. We can work to embrace that and find new beauty in every season of life. And as we do, we find those lovely pieces of life that reflect our true heart.

LOOK FOR LOVELY

Paint your nails today! Whether it is your first time EVER (start with a pink!) or you are addicted like me (add a signature nail!), today is the day for a little manicure. You could even choose a color that matches this book cover; I do that with each new book! As you are painting, use it as a time to pray and ask God what it would look like for you to cultivate a quiet and gentle spirit, to find for yourself what is healthy for your soul and your body.

And okay, if painting your nails just REALLY isn't your thing, find something you can do for your outside that reflects the work God is doing on the inside. I know a fresh haircut can sometimes work miracles. Maybe it's just a new lipstick color or pair of earrings. And remember while you're doing it that you're not trying to mask your insides. Pray that your outside would reflect the strength and beauty of who God has made you to be on the inside. Because it is beautiful.

Sushi

*For God is not a God of
disorder but of peace.*

—1 CORINTHIANS 14:33 NIV

A new place in downtown Athens, Georgia had just opened up. Utage is a sushi restaurant, right at the end of East Clayton Street. Caren and I decided to try it on a cold night in the winter. The leaves were all gone from the tree branches that arch over the main downtown street, but we found a close parking spot, so we just hopped out and ran inside, sadly not getting a chance to admire my favorite part of that street—the sparkly lights in the bare trees.

It was a big-deal adult dinner for us. No longer college students (by approximately five months), we were going out to dinner during the week to speak of our work woes and the challenges of being OH SO MATURE AND ADULT. So

111

clearly we needed sushi because that's what all the twenty-three-year-old working gals in the big city were eating tonight too.

Neither of us really knew how to order. Southern gals like us can hold our own in a barbecue restaurant or in a meat-and-three place. (That's a meat and three vegetables for you non-Southern readers. Or I should say a meat and three sides because coleslaw counts as a vegetable in the South. SO DOES MACARONI AND CHEESE. It's true.) But this sushi business was way out of our comfort zone. I read the menu and looked at the pictures. I had seen sushi before obviously but had never tasted it. So I didn't know what any of the rolls were going to be like. There was a lot I didn't know about this particular experience. I didn't know how much sushi I needed to call it a meal, but I was betting it was more than one roll. I wasn't sure what I would like and what I wouldn't like, though I was pretty certain raw-ness was not going to be my favorite. (This is a problem, as you probably know, because 90 percent of sushi rolls are raw.)

I also didn't know what the seaweed paper was going to do to my intestines. Ahem.

So we ordered to the best of our uneducated ability. We got edamame; that seemed safe enough. Healthy, simple, not mixed with raw ocean animals. At the waitress's suggestion, I got two rolls that night, one with crab and one with shrimp. I didn't love the taste of the seaweed, but the rest of the sushi experience was awesome.

But for the next two days, everything smelled and tasted like seaweed, and my stomach turned anytime I thought of it. Eventually, I was WHOA REALLY sick and never returned to the land of seaweed eating. In fact, I swore off sushi after that one experience in my college town because I was certain it was altogether poisonous.

That was until I moved to Nashville and told the story to my Bible study group. "No, no, no," Graham said, "let us take you to Samurai Sushi. It's the best in town, and you don't even have to have seaweed. You can ask for soy paper wraps instead."

Soy paper wraps? I couldn't believe it. For years I had been avoiding sushi because of the seaweed, and now there was another option. We went, and I let my friends order for me. A few minutes later, out came the most beautiful plate of food I had ever seen. The Hawaiian roll was spread out on the plate, the pale soy paper wrapped around the rice, fried shrimp, and asparagus, and it was all topped off with mango and peanuts. I had died and gone to Asian food heaven. The second roll they had ordered for me was the Happy Roll, similar to the Hawaiian but with crab and asparagus inside and kiwi on top.

The plate was so colorful. Reds and oranges, whites and greens. It looked like something that was drawn with big fat markers from your elementary school classroom.

And since that day, sushi has become a staple in my dietary life. I am still the wimpiest of all sushi eaters, leaning more toward shrimp and crab rolls, none of that raw salmon business, and certainly I steer clear of the scoop of fish eggs they can spread across the top of the rolls. But you can talk me into sushi just about any night of the week.

One night my friend Nichole texted to see if I wanted to meet her at Ginza, the small local sushi spot just around the corner from our houses. I didn't even have to think about my answer. I just asked how quickly she could get there because, yes, sushi was calling my name for dinner, that was for sure.

I pretty much wanted to be anywhere but at my house that night. Just weeks after returning from the beach trip where I had run from Matt to stare my broken crazy in the face, I was now back home, and though I was seeing a counselor, I couldn't seem to pull my life together. I washed clothes and left them in the dryer, just plucking from there anything that felt wearable. I used all the dishes, leaving dirty ones in the sink. I attempted to clean out some clothes and purge a bit, thinking a fresh start would help my mind, but it mainly just led to piles of clothes on the floor that I stepped over on the way to my bed every night. (I lived alone at the time—did I mention that? So I wasn't ruining anyone else's life but my own.)

So I had been there, in the messiest house, all day already, lying on the couch, watching television. It started innocently enough with a Men's World Cup soccer match that morning. Then I fell asleep, got up and had lunch, then was back on the couch, watching a movie. I felt like I blinked and it was dinnertime. In reality I watched about ten hours of television.

So I was ready to breathe some fresh air, eat something besides Honey Nut Chex, and see a human.

Nichole and I sat down in the first green booth on the left when you walk in the door of Ginza. We were both wearing shorts, as it was one hundred degrees outside, the dog days of a southern summer, so our bare legs stuck to the plastic booths. Hardly having to look at the menu, we ordered our usual— edamame to share, one roll and a bowl of white rice for her, two rolls for me.

We talked about normal things. I mentioned none of my broken crazy or how I had spent my entire day lying on the couch. She told me about her business and a phone call with her mom. I sat there pretty quiet, just trying to glaze over all the things I was feeling but didn't have a category for. As she spoke, we ate through the edamame, the peas popping easily out of their salty pods.

Within a few minutes the rolls (and rice) were delivered to the table, and our waiter refilled the water glasses we had both emptied. I looked down at my two rolls, and without warning, my eyes were blurred with tears.

The rolls were beautiful. And orderly. And colorful. And natural.

I saw God in those sushi rolls. I saw how He is a God who puts everything in its right place.

For God is not a God of disorder but of peace.
—1 Corinthians 14:33

Each piece of the roll was symmetrical. There wasn't anything artificial in there. It was all real and orderly, and it made me cry because I saw the lovely, and I wanted it in my life. It felt like God whispered something into my heart about seeing how He does things and trying to be like Him. He wasn't out to shame my broken crazy or make me feel like I was a bad person. I think He just wanted me to see the beauty of order.

I went home after dinner and loaded the dishwasher. Then I folded that one half-load of clothes that had been sitting in the dryer. Don't get it twisted; I didn't do some massive overhaul of my life that night. I just came home and put two rather simple areas of my life in order. One for each roll I had for dinner, I suppose. That tiny bit of lovely set my night on a healthier track.

I now pick sushi on days when things feel out of bounds or when life feels messy because I found what I was looking for there, even if I didn't realize how much I was looking. I found lovely. I found God. I saw Him there and I still do.

I see the God who likes to put things back together. He loves to take ugly, messy things (and people) and make sense from the chaos. The fancy Bible word for that is *redemption*. I'm always amazed at how messy the lives are of the characters in the Bible. And I'm not just talking about the "bad guys" here. I'm talking the heroes of your Backyard Bible Club stories. Far from perfect, their stories are filled with lapses in judgment to rival any Hollywood movie plot. They're doubters, liars, idolaters, and schemers, even murderers.

God takes them all and knows exactly what to do with them. He knows how to take the crazy and give it significance. He knows how to take the oh-so-much-less-than-perfect and make it lovely. He's done it for me.

My life gets pretty hectic at times. I love it and I'm grateful, but road life can take its toll. One day, I got home from about fifteen days straight of speaking on the road, driving from city to city, and I had one night in Nashville before flying to Austin for my next speaking event. I immediately asked my girls if we could please go to Virago. It's way too fancy for a normal sushi dinner (that's why we have Ginza), but when a Virago request is made, people understand the situation. This isn't a normal day; this is an especially exciting or especially hard day. And this one felt especially hard. Road life isn't always easy for me, particularly when I feel like I'm missing out on friend time, so this one day when I have literally one meal in town with my friends made my job feel costly, and it made me feel sad, and I felt like life was very messy.

I threw on my glitter flats and met the girls in the Gulch at Virago. They sat us in a booth toward the back, and I sat quietly as my friends caught one another up on their days and dates and dreams. I wasn't trying to be uninvolved; I just wanted to hear them, watch them, be with them; and I wanted to save my voice because I had done a lot of talking lately on stages.

We started with crispy rice spicy tuna, the only almost raw thing I will eat in a sushi restaurant and the actual reason we go to Virago. It's an oval of rice, fried, and then topped with a tiny scoop of spicy raw tuna. Then they set the rolls on watermelon Pop Rocks. HOW WEIRD AND PERFECT IS THAT? We shared that appetizer, but for my main course I ordered The Bomb with soy paper. That roll is so expensive in calories and dollars that I cannot even talk about it. It has crab and shrimp and asparagus (can you sense a theme in my sushi taste?) and gold flakes or something because I have to dip into my savings account anytime I want to eat it. But it is oh. so. worth. it. The taste is near perfection, especially with a few drops of soy sauce. It came out, and I looked at it for a minute before I dug in.

I knew what I needed to see. The order. The colors. The peace. The Pop Rocks. I knew if I looked, I could find lovely in that sushi roll. Every time I order a roll these days, my mind immediately thinks back to Ginza with Nichole and how I saw, for the first time, God using sushi to remind me of His sovereign hand. So on a night like that, just a few hours of being with my girlfriends, just one night in my own bed, the sushi brought me peace. God is ordering my steps, God is ordering all things, and I rest in that.

LOOK FOR LOVELY

If you've never tried sushi, TODAY IS YOUR DAY! Go big and raw and fishy, or don't and sushi like me. But tonight for dinner, why not grab a roll or two? But before you eat it, look at it. Really look at it. See the colors and the symmetry and the way it is beautiful. Maybe God wants to remind you of something in that roll tonight.

And when you're done with that, go home—to your dorm room or apartment or parents' basement—and put some things in order. It can be as simple as getting all your school books off the floor and gathered up for the next day. It could be laundry. Maybe you need to make your bed. Yes, even after you get home from your fabulous sushi dinner, it's not too late to make your bed. A life of lovely is about putting the pieces together one little bit at a time. It's about finding the pieces that matter and will last. Sometimes that means doing things that feel silly like making your bed right before you're ready to pull those covers back again for some much-needed sleep. That's okay. Perseverance is one day at a time, even one minute at a time on our worst days.

So find the thing today, right in front of you, that will bring order to your life. Thank God that He is ordering all things and has ordered all things. He didn't just jump on the job yesterday. He's always been in the business of making sense out of our broken crazy.

Yellow and Blue

*Live in harmony with
one another.*

—ROMANS 12:16 NIV

When I was in the youth group, our church had a family serving as missionaries in the heart of Paris, France. Thanks to them we had the unique opportunity to spend our high school spring break weeks in Paris, partnering with them in ministry and sharing the gospel. We stayed in host homes, we did musical performances around town that told the story of Jesus, and I grew to love Paris. It didn't feel romantic or like home to me; it just always felt comfortable.

I love all the special spots in Paris—Notre Dame, the tiny crepe place just beside Notre Dame, Sacré-Coeur, Montmartre, Versailles and the queen's quarters behind it. The only thing I do not love, and I like to complain about given the chance, is the Louvre.

Now listen. I like art. I really do. And large paintings that span across a room absolutely take my breath away.

But the Louvre? I do not like it. When I was a teenager, they took my book bag from me as I entered, making me "check" it with the coats, leaving me without my water bottle or my camera, and I was totally undone. And apparently I still hold a grudge many years later. (I should give it another run, probably. But I'm not quite ready to do that yet.)

I also have so much eye roll for the *Mona Lisa*. She's tiny and crowded. You can hardly get up next to her to see her, and once you do, it's like, "Eh, okay, I saw it. What now?" And then her eyes follow you around the room, and it's wicked creepy.

After I graduated high school, my family saved up money, and we took a trip to London and Paris. Sally was just nine or ten. Tatum and I were high schoolers. At this point I had spent three spring breaks in Paris, so returning with my family felt like I was showing them around a town I thought I knew. Our main goal, the big highlight, was hanging out with the DeJarnett family, the ones who were there serving as missionaries.

One day we decided to take a day trip to Giverny, where famous painter Claude Monet's home still stands. My mom is a longtime art fan, and I had grown to love it as well (except for the *Mona Lisa*, obviously), and so I was really excited for this excursion. It was only about an hour's drive from where we were staying in Jouy-en-Josas to Giverny, so we loaded up the rental car and headed northwest, past Versailles, toward the suburb where the house stood.[6]

We arrived, and the line to buy a ticket to tour the home and gardens was twenty or so people deep. Sally had stayed back with the DeJarnetts to ride bikes with their daughter Marie-Claire, so it was just the four of us—Mom, Dad, Tatum, and me. I don't know what the tour is like now, but in 1998 you didn't get to see many rooms, and you could not take any pictures. But I didn't need to—the interior of the house is strong in my memory.

The tour mainly focuses on five or six rooms on the main floor of the home. Monet picked all the paint colors, the tour guide told us, and each was intentional based on the natural light, the wood, and the decor he wanted to put in the room. As the tour guide led us into the dining room, she pointed out the color on the walls. The room was sunny yellow on every wall. Very simple, but two tones of really perfect dining-room yellows. It felt like the shades that would set people at ease and feel fresh year round. The glassware in the room, in the china cabinets and on all the shelves, was blue. Bright blue.

While we were still standing there, on the rust red-and-white checkered floors, she pointed through the dining room into the kitchen. You could only see through a wide doorway, but the kitchen was a beautiful soft blue. Blue-and-white tiles, plus the natural light coming through the windows that we could not see, combined to give the doorway almost a hazy blue feel. And then when we stood in the blue kitchen and looked into the dining room, the brightness of the yellow was so inviting and fun.

It wasn't just about the yellow of the dining room, she explained. It was about the yellow when you also saw the blue of the kitchen. It made both colors better, brighter, and more impactful when they were combined. So Monet picked the two colors of these rooms to complement each other and to take what was already lovely and make it even lovelier. A website about the home, created by the city of Giverny, says, "Monet wanted a blue kitchen so that the guests would see the right color in harmony with the yellow dining room when the door to the kitchen was open."[7]

Yes. The harmony. I felt that.

Every color was picked not only for its own values but also for how it would look in connection with the other rooms around it. I just kept popping back and forth between the two rooms, even after the tour group began to move from the house to the gardens, where the water lilies pond still exists. (And seriously, it looks exactly like Monet's series of water lilies paintings. It's incredible.)

I think about these two rooms all the time, and I've spent significant brain space over the years trying to decorate my home in harmonizing blues and yellows. I can't forget how those colors, while truly beautiful on their own, were actually far more stunning together. Though super different, the way these colors cooperated impacted me.

Nichole, my sushi-eating friend, is one of my best friends in Nashville. (You didn't miss some transition paragraph that accidentally got deleted. Hang with me, and you'll see the connection between Nichole and Monet.)

Nichole is from the North; Ohio, to be precise. She probably wouldn't call it the North, but where I come from, Ohio is absolutely the North.

(I am from the South.)

Nichole was an elite-level gymnast as a child and still cries when she watches the Olympic Games because she feels so connected to the sport. She was also a Division I level college athlete in swimming.

(When I was in college, I went to the University of Georgia workout facility about once a month and took bowling as my college physical education class.)

Nichole is a CPA and honors the power of numbers and balance sheets and dollar signs.

(I don't like to live by a budget because I feel like I'm being bullied.)

Nichole is often more quiet and reserved, choosing to listen and ask questions.

(I'm Annie. I'm loud. Always.)

If someone needs a wing woman, if one of us is having to go somewhere alone and wishes we had a friend to go with us,

Nichole is always that girl. It actually doesn't matter to Nichole whether she knows the other people at the event or not. In fact, more often than not, Nichole does not want to go to the event in question, but if one of her friends needs her, she shows up.

(I tend to shy away from doing things I don't want to do. On the selfish scale, I'm on it.)

She doesn't give up. I've watched her struggle with the business she owns, struggle with questions in her faith, struggle with her health, family issues, and hurts. And yet she doesn't give up.

(I'm a quitter.)

We are very different. We share a few things, like our faith and enjoyment of sushi and swimming pools, but if you just looked at the stats, if you just looked at our histories, you would never put us together.

Like blue. And yellow.

But something happens when we stand by each other. My loud brings beauty to her quiet, and her quiet brings beauty to my loud. My selfishness really displays her consistent willingness to be a wing woman, and her generosity really makes my selfishness, um, stand out. Her northernness mixes with my southernness; and though we don't always understand each other's upbringing (WHY DO YOU SAY POP FOR COKE?), I appreciate her shade of culture, and she appreciates mine. We look better together than apart. She adds value to my life, and next to me, she makes me a more beautiful Annie.

It's like a body with lots of parts, isn't it? Like it says in 1 Corinthians 12, there is so much benefit from the parts working together. Blue and yellow, Annie and Nichole, an arm and a leg. Our differences are clear, but the ways we can work together far surpass the need to focus on ways we aren't alike.

This is why we can't be friends only with folks who look and act just like us. When I moved to Nashville, I initially set out to make friends with people who reminded me of my friends from home. Similar upbringing, similar college experience, similar faith journey. It's easier that way, to know and be known, just as it is easier to paint two rooms the same shade of blue. But as I met men and women who weren't like me—Nichole is a perfect example—my mind expanded. And it just kept happening— becoming friends with people who were not at all like me. Because of the melting pot of Nashville, and people moving in to this city from every corner of the map, finding someone from metro Atlanta who was also a Georgia Bulldog became less simple and honestly, less important.

It's so exciting to talk to you about this and to think about the stage of life that you're in. If you're in college or even starting out in the scary-adult-work-world, you're figuring out how to make new friends left and right. So many of the friends we find along the way come through way of convenience—you're in class together, you're in a study group together, you work the same shift at Chili's together, you go on a mission trip together.

Maybe you didn't plan on being friends; it just happened. Sometimes those are the best kind.

Are you only looking around for the people who look and talk and act just like your high school friends? Keep those eyes wide open to the people you cross paths with that might be the least likely friendship candidates. Don't write someone off because you only see the differences at first. You'll find some of the richest friendships in life are sometimes the ones that never would have happened if you had only been looking for people exactly like you.

It's why, at times, the best thing you can do when you meet someone new is to look past all the differences and instead focus on what you share. Because we don't need to just be like us forever. There are parts of my hue that would improve if I were more like Nichole, and there may be times my friendship helps her as well. But had we looked at each other five years ago when we met and just went with what we saw at first glance, we'd have thought our colors were too different to stand together well. I'm glad we didn't quit then. I'm glad when we saw my blue and her yellow, we didn't walk away and set out for me to find more blues and for her to find more yellows.

Monet's house taught me something valuable that has stuck with me for almost two decades. I see it working in my life and I thank God for Monet, for yellow and blue, and for Nichole.

LOOK FOR LOVELY

Which friend in your life is different from you? Call her today, and thank her for all the ways her uniqueness complements your own. Maybe this is also a good time to make a new friend, someone who seems different from you, someone you have avoided because you were certain the commonalities couldn't override the differences. Younger, older, someone from a different culture, race, or religious background. Make that extra effort to reach out beyond your current circle and get to know that person you've maybe seen or spoken to in passing.

And you know this challenge comes with the extra bonus of blessing someone else in the process. You never know what that other girl is going through. Maybe she needs a new friend today, too, but is afraid to take the first step. Maybe she's going through something super hard and doesn't have anyone to talk to. Maybe you'll be exactly the friend she needed but didn't know how to find. You just never know.

My People

Every time you cross my mind,
I break out in exclamations of
thanks to God. Each exclamation
is a trigger to prayer. I find myself
praying for you with a glad heart.

—PHILIPPIANS 1:3-4 MSG

 Going to the University of Georgia was one of the best decisions of my life. Not only did I love wearing red and black and living in Athens, Georgia, but it's also the time in my life when I think I learned the most about God. I loved being a part of the Wesley Foundation, one of the campus ministries at UGA. I was discipled by an older female student who taught me a lot about prayer. I was in small groups where friendships grew and we worshiped and prayed together, and I went on some of the most influential mission trips that shaped the rest of my life. But it wasn't the trips or the programs so much that shaped me, but the people who were part of the journey. The experiences were influential. The people were absolutely life-changing.

I led a small group of college girls here in Nashville for almost four years. I love young women (hence, you know, this book). Transition, new experiences, new friendships, heartbreaks, learning all about who you are and who God says you are. What an amazing and formative time of life. When I moved home to Nashville after doing college ministry in Edinburgh, Scotland, for six months, I knew I was moving home with the hope of getting involved in the lives of college students here in town.

My church had a service that was focused on college students at the time, and that's where I was introduced to the little crew of gals that started meeting at my house. At the beginning, in those first few weeks when we sat in a circle in my living room, I had a basket of questions that we passed around each week, and each girl had to pull a question and answer it.

What are you afraid of?

What's your favorite dessert?

Dream vacation location?

Why did you join this small group?

We covered a whole gamut of things every week just in the opening questions. We always ate dinner together—in fact, I feel like I have really become quite competent in cooking meals for twelve. My girls eat like they are college male athletes, so I rarely have much left over. If I do, they always congregate back in the kitchen after group and grab baggies and scavenge any crumbs that might remain.

Before I became allergic to dairy and before I quit gluten, we ate a lot of casseroles. If there is one thing a Southern girl learns as she is growing up, it is how to use cream of chicken soup to combine meat and vegetables, even though I can't really tell you what cream of chicken is (and what I imagine it is grosses me out). So I've known how to make casseroles—breakfast or dinner—for the entirety of my life. It came in handy when I was trying to feed a crowd. But then once my eating changed, so did the casserole opportunities. No longer able to mix sour cream with chicken and carrots, I had to find other alternatives. No longer serving ice cream bars, I had to come up with desserts that were healthy (or healthy-ish) for the girls. As my eating changed, so did what the gals ate every Tuesday night.

It usually went pretty well, especially when I asked Pinterest to help me find a new recipe. "Feeding the 12" became the board I populated the most, loading it with big family recipes, because I thought the title was hilariously witty, and I needed help feeding all the people. I remember only one meal being a complete failure. Sure, Hannah didn't like the weeks I served fish, and April always cringed if she even SENSED there was a mushroom in the building, but the only total failure was the Crock-Pot baked potatoes. I promise I followed the rules exactly as Pinterest told me—wrapping them each in aluminum foil, stacking them in the Crock-Pot, leaving it on *alllll* day long.

When it was time to eat, they were mostly cooked through, but they were a weird color. And each one tasted like metal, as if the aluminum foil infused the potato. I thought for sure I'd lose some girls after that meal. Gratefully, everyone came back the next Tuesday.

But in my heart I knew even bad cooking wouldn't keep them from our Tuesday nights. In their first semester as freshmen, we made a decision as a group. We were going to stick it out until they graduated. There were a few older girls in there, but the majority were the same class, so we decided that whatever we were starting here, we were going to see to the end.

I need people like that in my life. I need people who are committed to staying. It helps me commit too—to being honest, to being present, to allowing people into the corners that tend to stay dark and hidden. I'm willing to show people the corners if they plan to stay. And that's who we became for one another, every Tuesday night of the school year for four years in a row.

We had an understanding among our group—say what you need to say, ask what you need to ask, because we aren't going anywhere. When Anne and Melissa got in a fight over roommate issues, we sat on my couch together, and they both said the real stuff and survived it. When Karen got her feelings hurt by Heather and Jennifer, I made pancakes, and we all sat in my living room while maple syrup and tears poured. But they survived it. When Brandi felt attacked because no one liked her boyfriend, she was hurt, but she survived it.

A couple of girls moved away, but none of them quit. That's the thing. There were multiple arguments, hard conversations, tears were a weekly occurrence (but so was dessert), and we studied the Bible and prayed and listened to God and worshipped. We did lots of things, but we never quit.

I think of Exodus 17. Moses sent Joshua out to fight the Amalekites. As Joshua was out in the battle, if Moses's hands were raised, the Israelite army was winning. Any time he put his hands down because his arms were tired, the Amalekites advanced. So while Moses stood at the top of the hill watching the battle below, his brother Aaron and his brother-in-law Hur came and held up his arms. They stayed by him, holding up his arms, until the sunset. All. Day. Long.

I love that visual. Having the people in your life who will hold you up when you are too tired to keep doing what you are called to do. Remembering that Moses got tired takes away some of the guilt I feel when I am tired. Moses didn't try to do everything on his own. In fact, in Exodus 18, his father-in-law reminded Moses again that he couldn't do it all in his own strength; it was too much for one man to carry. He had to persevere to ensure there was a victory—he had to keep his hands up even when he felt like he was unable to do it anymore—but he couldn't do it alone. He needed his people.

My girls grew to need one another like that. It was beautiful to watch, painful at times, frustrating more than I probably want to admit, and many weeks, exhausting. But so beautiful. And I needed them too. I love my people, and I'm pretty eyes wide-open to the ones God brings into my life to stand beside me and hold up my arms and whose arms I want to hold up as well. And those girls are that for me and for one another.

I have a group text with my lifelong best friends—Haley, Molly, and Misti. Group texting is such a victory for us because we are now able to communicate pretty much constantly. Whether it is needing help with relationships or recipe suggestions or real deep hurts and PLEASE PRAY NOWs, or ridiculous gifs, we are always there for each other.

When I need to say the really honest thing, when I need to spew my frustrations, I go to them. I'm not afraid to complain about being single or about missing a flight or about some family drama because I know they aren't going anywhere. They aren't scared of me or my issues. I know we are committed to one another, as best we can be for as long as we can be.

The beauty of growing up in Marietta, Georgia, but living in Nashville, Tennessee, is that it is only a three-and-a-half-hour drive between the two cities. A few months ago one of them had a family emergency, and I was able to be there in just a few hours, with a strawberry cake in hand, ready to sit on the floor with the three of them and cry and eat cake until we were almost sick.

And when my broken crazy got bad, I told them. While I was still on that beach trip, lying by the pool, I texted them all and told them the truth. The next week Molly rode a bus all the way to Nashville just to be with me in it. Just to hold my arms up. It wasn't an intervention or a big deal; she just didn't want me to be alone.

People can be that for you.

When I first moved to Nashville, the friends I met made the move bearable.

When I first moved to Edinburgh, Scotland, the part that kept me from massive homesickness was the people that invited me into their lives.

When I travel to speak, I almost always bring a friend with me because that's what makes me feel the most normal and the most Annie.

When I traveled to Israel, I came home with a few new life-long friends.

God keeps using humans in my life to help me keep going. Whether it's the friends on the plane reminding me to fix my life when the broken crazy got so bad, or my counselor, or the friends on Instagram reminding me that finishing a book really matters, I feel like God sets all those people on the side of the road as I am running my race.

I ran a half marathon once. I talk about it a lot because I've only done it once, and I only plan to do it once. It was 13.1 miles of chafing torture. Five of my friends also ran it, but they were in much better shape and much faster runners, so with my blessing, they left me in the dust before the first mile was even completed.

Right as I started mile twelve, over three hours into the race, I noticed someone running toward me. I was part walking / part jogging / part barely surviving, and this young woman was coming straight toward me. It took me a minute to realize it was my friend, Katie. Katie had finished the race over an hour before. But here she was, beginning at the finish line and running the course backward until she found me. (Is that even allowed? I'm sure she was breaking some kind of half-marathon rule.)

I asked her what in the world she was doing. "I just came back to finish with you," she said with a smile. I couldn't believe it. Katie ran an extra 2.2 miles just to find me and help me finish. She encouraged me as we ran, as we finished together. She didn't let me quit; she didn't even let me walk when I wanted to walk. She just kept telling me how glad I would be when we finished.

I'll never forget that. I'll never forget that Katie sacrificed her own comfort to hold my arms up in a time of need, when I don't know that I would have gotten victory on my own.

I'm a people person. I'm always extroverted, and I barely know a stranger. But more than just a person who likes humans, I'm particularly a MY people person. I absolutely love my friends and family. I believe you are shaped by the people you surround yourself with, and I am deeply shaped by the people around me.

I spend the most time with our little group of single girls here in Nashville. There are about ten of us, and we all speak the same language. We all believe in God and one another. We all have found careers we love and a class at the gym we love. We eat out too much and travel together often. The best part of a group text between ten people is if you send out a "Who wants to get BBQ for dinner?" there's a chance that at least one person will be available. Sometimes, rarely, it's all of us. But usually at least three of us decide to eat together, or see a movie, or fly to Albuquerque for a Lady Antebellum show.

If you're thinking, "Wow, Annie's life sounds so great!" Well, you'd be right! (Wink, wink.) No, I'm not bragging. I've already told you about my ups and downs and everything in between. I've already told you about the struggle. What I want you to hear is I'm making it through the struggle in large part thanks to these women and friends who surround me. I couldn't have done it without them. It's not just what we do together, it's who we are for each other.

These women are great for fun. But they are also great when things aren't great. We've cried together over breakups and heartache and job failures and family pain. In a world that works hard to make us feel alone in our singleness, we lock arms and refuse to hear it. We are not alone.

You need someone to remind you of that. And sometimes it feels like we have no one. Whether it's scrolling through Instagram and seeing what you are missing out on or not knowing whom to call when you need a voice on the other side, it can feel like this planet is very lonely. I get that. I feel that at times too.

Did you know that depression and anxiety among teenagers and college students is at an all-time high? Studies show anywhere from 1 in 5 to 1 in 3 college students now struggle with depression. We would be naïve to try to point a finger at only one cause, but experts know without a doubt that one of the reasons for this rise in anxiety and other mental-health issues is that little piece of metal and technology we hold in our hands every day called a smartphone. And more specifically, that beauty and beast called social media. It's a magical thing that connects us to friends and family near and far and also reminds us too often that we might be missing out, left out, uninvited, or just plain forgotten. It makes us lonely. We need real life, flesh-and-blood friends, to keep reminding us we ARE NOT ALONE.

When I first moved to Nashville, I had acquaintances but no friends. And in that season is when it became very real to me that Jesus could be a Friend who sticks closer than a brother (Proverbs 18:24). It's not like someone sat with me at dinner, but something beautiful happened when I started asking Him to be my Friend, my close Friend. While I was still alone, and while we aren't meant to do life by ourselves, Jesus stepped into an empty spot in my heart. And then, as I made friends and these circles of relationships grew, I was so grateful for the season when He solidified His spot as my closest Friend.

My small-group girls, my Marietta besties, my single gals in Nashville. They are the ones who hold my hands up, who come back to where I'm struggling in any kind of race and help me finish. And they are the ones I run toward as well. This journey of life brings us lots of different kinds of friends. Your friends from high school may not always be in the picture. Maybe they will. You'll have seasonal friends—the ones who come and go like fall leaves making room for new growth in spring. That's not bad. Embrace them for the time they're in your life; then make room for new friends.

Then you'll have lifers. The ones who won't go away even if you tried to push them away. Hold on as tight as you can to those.

It's not about the number of people you have; it's just about having even one person who can hold your arms up when things get hard. Don't you dare believe the lie that more friends on Snapchat or more followers on Instagram means someone else is loved more than you. If you have one person—ONE—who will walk alongside you and hold up your arms, count yourself blessed. It could be your mom or your sister or your coworker. It could be your small group or softball team. It could be your best friend or your twenty best friends.

Our last gathering with that group of college girls was on a Tuesday night in April. The girls were all stressed and busy, trying to get all their senior projects turned in. I made them dinner, and I cried while I bought the groceries. When the girls arrived, an awkward heaviness hung over us. This was really it; we were ending. They loaded up their plates with grilled chicken and all piled into the living room, sliding into their usual seats on the sofas and on the floor. We talked for a bit about what was next and what we had meant to one another. This was their chance, I told them. We didn't need an emotional scene necessarily, but this was the last time we'd be like this; and if they had things to say to one another, if they wanted to express their love or gratitude, this was the time.

And they did. It was beautiful and personal and demonstrated that every bit of the time they'd invested to hold one another's arms high in the air was worth it. I told them what I still believe is true. We didn't do relationship perfectly, but we did right by this group and by one another. We did that right.

We prayed, and as I said, "Amen," no one spoke. We all sat right where we were and wept those quiet tears that remind you that it all mattered.

I'll never forget that night. I'll never forget those girls, and that's not just because a group picture is framed in my living room. I won't forget them because they taught me, like Haley and Misti and Molly have, like Katie did when she ran back to help me finish, that without your people, without letting them in and letting them know you, you won't be able to persevere. Your people remind you of the goodness of God and remind you of what it means to finish.

LOOK FOR LOVELY

Who is your person? Who holds your arms up? Find them, thank them, hug them. Whose arms are you holding up?

Has anyone talked to you about getting a mentor? This is a beautiful thing. It's incredible to have these real friends in your life who say the real things, the hard things. But what about an older woman who's been there and done that, so to speak? Do you have anyone like that? After you've hugged your people, think about a woman in your life who can hold your arms up in a different way. Not as a peer or a fellow journeyer, but as a person who has blazed the trail before you. Someone who has persevered and lived to tell the tale. Ask her to sit with you and tell her story. Ask her to be part of your story.

And one more thing. I don't want to walk away from this chapter without recognizing my friend who might be reading this and thinking, "I don't have a person." I love you, friend. I hurt with you. Can you start by letting Jesus be that closest Friend for you? Then, can I challenge you to be brave? Find a person. Be that friend for someone else that you want someone to be for you.

Lightning Bug

pray for the peace of Jerusalem.

—PSALM 122:6 NIV

 After more than a week in Israel, we spent our last night in Tel Aviv. There were about thirty of us from cities across the USA. Many of us were strangers before the trip, but it was one of those events that binds people together in a unique way. So they each became that real kind of friend you want to hang on to forever and frame pictures of across your entire house. (Or maybe that's just me? I am quite sentimental.)

We ate a late dinner at the hotel. Then a lot of us walked down to the restaurant that was across the street on the beach of the Mediterranean Sea. This seaside spot bordered off its tables with red skinny pyramid lights, about five feet in height, all lit up. We grabbed a bunch of chairs and tables, circled them up, and sat down. I walked to the edge of the sea and waded into the pitch-black water, only about two feet in, because I didn't want to get eaten by a sea animal at night, but I definitely wanted to touch the Mediterranean.

At this point, eight days in with only one to go, I was beginning to mourn the loss of this time together. The breeze was blowing, and my hair was getting sea salty. It was still warm outside, even though it was almost midnight, but I felt happy not to be sweating anymore. I listened to my guy friends talk but also tried to breathe in the moment and look around and almost memorize every detail of what was going on. The simplicity of sitting around a table on the beach with Ryan and Matthew and Ross, hearing Jessica and Jon talking over my shoulder, watching some of the other guys swimming in the ocean, seeing Grant and Kim swapping stories. I wanted to memorize it, begging my mind not to forget the red haze of the pyramid lights or the menu that was in Hebrew and English, what everyone was wearing and drinking and saying. I wanted to remember it all, and I was terrified that I wouldn't be able to.

I knew that the next night we'd all be getting on an airplane, and after flying eleven hours, we'd land in America and all go our separate ways—back to our homes, our families, our cities—and we would never be here, like this, again. And that broke my heart, even while I was still sitting around the circle with my friends. I'm weird like that. I get super sad about something ending before it ever ends. Instead of appreciating a lightning bug when it is illuminating the night, I watch it and get sad about when it will go away. Maybe this is why, as a kid, I always collected lightning bugs in mason jars. I wanted to collect and hold all those bright moments and never let them go. But sometimes they go, they leave, they stop. I started to feel panic, sitting on that beach, like I was watching the lightning bugs lose their twinkle as the minutes ticked away.

I thought about how I almost didn't go on this trip. To be honest, I've always been a little afraid to go to Israel. Fear isn't often a guiding emotion for me, but when I listened to the news and read online about Israel, it always seemed to be getting bombed.

I try not to go places that are getting bombed.

So in 2014, when Josh from the Israel Collective reached out to me, first via e-mail and then in a phone call, and offered for me to join a team that was going to Israel, I thought it sounded cool, but I mainly thought it sounded dangerous, so I said no thanks.

Six months later I changed my mind, and in September 2015, I went to Israel with thirty people I did not know.

But it only took eight days to feel like they were my people and like some part of me never wanted this trip to end. (And, just a note, I felt absolutely safe the entire time.) I'm a physical touch person, and in situations like this, sitting on the beach in Tel Aviv, when my foot kicked Matthew because he made a dumb joke or I high-fived Ross because I absolutely agree that doughnuts are a food group, I started to mourn because I knew this was what I was going to lose when we all returned home. We could FaceTime and phone chat and text every waking hour, but physical presence would be gone.

As the night wore on, conversations continued, and people headed slowly back to the hotel, one or two at a time. I was also running out of steam. I was so tired, and we still had another full day ahead of us before we were scheduled to fly out, but I didn't want to miss one minute with my friends. My eyelids were drooping; the guys who remained were all still wide-awake. So I knew I had to go to bed, but I was just so sad about it. Because it was the end.

When you collect the moments that matter, it means the moments have passed. And that's sometimes hard for me. I see the value in them, clearly, and the importance of remembering what it felt like to slide my feet in that sand and listen to the guys talk about theology and tacos and Texas; and recalling that memory, even today, strengthens me.

Why do I still feel sad today, at home in Nashville, and yet smile when I think of that night on the beach? How can that be? How can sadness and joy coexist? How can a memory that makes me so happy also be a memory that brings sadness?

Paul was so faithful in his letters from prison to remind the churches, always in the first few sentences, of how he was thanking God for them and their partnership in spreading the gospel. Paul was pulling strength from those memories of friends and stories he continued to hear, even though he wasn't with them, even while imprisoned.

As you know, I'm a pain avoider, and yet I have a bad habit of tossing out the memories I need because they also hurt. But I've realized there is something beautiful, and something that opens your heart in new and deeper ways, when you open yourself up to experience pain as well as joy. I think that has to be part of all of this. Maybe that's what it means to rejoice in our sufferings as Paul says in Romans 5? Maybe when we make our hearts available to the hard moments and allow ourselves to experience God's love in new ways, we are also increasing our capacity to love others.

I feel that with these new friends. At the end of a two-year journey toward mental and physical and spiritual health, here are these guys who are meeting Post-Broken Crazy Annie. I am more open and braver and kinder because I remember the pain of the broken crazy, and I remember all the things that led to the breakdown, and while I don't relish any new pain, I don't put it in a box and shove it into the back corner of my heart, either. There is a chance I love them more because of what has transpired over the last few years. And that's not about them; that's about me.

Ryan and Ross and Matthew walked me back to the hotel because it was getting late, and I didn't want to star in any television show about an author being abducted in Tel Aviv. So, they were my bodyguards. We called the elevator, and while waiting, we turned around toward the mirrored wall and took a picture. I have the picture hanging above my desk, and I see it every day as I write: My hair is plastered to my head, and my jeans are rolled up and soaked to the knee. Matthew's hat is pushed back; he's wearing a black compression sleeve under his white T-shirt because of a pre-trip injury. Ryan and Ross are both holding their tennis shoes in their hands, and Ryan has a beach towel thrown over his shoulder. Matthew is taking the picture, so we're all turned toward him. Our faces all say the same thing with different looks, but we are all expressing something about how we feel just standing there with one another.

When the elevator arrived that night in Tel Aviv, I said good night and took the elevator to the fourth floor. I walked into my room, and before the door was even closed behind me, I was crying. I cried because I was scared. I was scared that when this trip was over, the friendships were going to end as well. You've probably been to enough summer camps to know what happens when you are there and when you are home, and I didn't want it to happen, that slow fade of communication. I was scared I was going to lose them when we got home, and I was scared of that loss, and I was scared I wouldn't know what to do with my fear. It all felt new to me, maybe because parts of my heart are new, so I was feeling the new parts of my heart break. It was my lightning bug fear manifesting in friendships I didn't want to blink out.

I'm sure you can relate. You've probably left a lot of friends behind in recent years, not by choice but just by sheer geography. Some you knew for years like high-school friends or college friends. Some came and went quickly like my Tel Aviv friends. They were camp friends or mission-trip friends or cheerleading squad friends. They had a special place in time that won't ever happen again.

I was scared that collecting those moments would feel like trying to hold onto bubbles or wind or ice cream. I was scared the tighter I tried to grip the more I'd panic, and those moments would slip through my fingers, and while I was freaking out about losing them, they would be gone.

I said as much to the Lord that night in Tel Aviv. I started with thanks because I couldn't believe He let us all travel together and kept us safe, but then I told Him I was worried and scared. I told Him I didn't know how to collect memories I wish weren't stories with endings. I asked Him how to do this, how to navigate these new healthy heart moments that felt so deeply sad.

And I felt like He asked me to trust Him. To let Him hold the things my hands cannot grasp. I think that may be the trick to this whole life of lovely business. I think confessing to God when it seems hard or scary or painful, confessing what you want to do but what feels too challenging—it's what helps you keep building. It's what helps you see Him in the people you meet and in the moments when you have to let them leave.

While I collect moments, He will collect friendships and make them last. And whether that friendship remains a physical presence in my life, I can let the memory of it be another brick on the foundation of this life He's building. If you look back over those significant moments—the week at camp, the trip with your mom, the weekend you went white-water rafting—you can start to see the pieces come together, can't you? You start to see how He has used each of those moments that have come and gone to transform you into you.

I decided to believe that's what God was doing that night in Tel Aviv. He was laying down another brick. I believe that He is who holds all things together, including that squad, those memories, my heart. My phone beeped that night in my hotel room as Matthew texted over that picture. As I stared at it, I knew that for months and years to come, this one simple photograph would be my lightning bug that would never go out.

LOOK FOR LOVELY

Pull out some old photos and look at the people. What did they mean to you? How did they matter? Which folks could you reach out to today and tell them what they mean to you?

It's a practice that maybe is a little lost in these days of hyper-technology. Talking to each other face-to-face, that is. Telling the people who matter the most exactly how much they matter and why. Let's bring it back.

Gardens

He has made everything beautiful in its time. He has also set eternity in the human heart; yet no one can fathom what God has done from beginning to end.

—ECCLESIASTES 3:11 NIV

I laced up my mint-and-gray tennis shoes and threw on my raincoat. It had rained all day in New York City, and by 1:00 p.m., it was barely slowing down. I had been sitting at the desk in this tiny apartment, rented on Airbnb, for the entire morning, writing. It was time to let my legs do some work while my fingers and brain rested. I didn't have a real destination, except I wanted a smoothie from a lime-green storefront on East 9th Street and 1st Avenue. I walked toward Tompkins Square Park, mainly because Mumford and Sons wrote an entire song about it, so I tried to go past it at least once a day during my stay. I kept walking, Hillsong United in my earbuds, until I realized I was almost to the East River. Oops.

Time to turn around. At Avenue C, headed back west, I made a left-hand turn off of 10th and decided to go ahead and hop on 9th to go up toward the smoothie.

Looking down at my phone to answer a text message, I crossed over Avenue C and started walking up 9th Avenue. To my left, I spotted a garden. I put my phone back in the raincoat pocket and slowed my pace to look more closely. Huge weeping willow trees flung their branches over the fence and onto the sidewalk, creating a little protection from the rain. I could look through the fence to see a beautiful and well-kept garden, full of plants and benches and stone paths. And though I couldn't quite see the fullness of it, was that an amphitheater back there? I think it was.

Across the top of the chain-link fence were these multicolored flowers of all sizes and shades, made from old cans and bottles. The cans had been cut into strips, from top to bottom, while still being attached to the base. Then the strips were curled outward, like petals on a flower. Some different-colored bottle caps and such were used for the center of the flowers. It was just old trash, treasured, folded around, and turned into something beautiful. And there were so many of them, all tightly bundled together like bouquets or fields or those cases of flowers in grocery stores. It stretched for half the block or so.

I lingered at the garden's fence, watching the lone rooster that was just on the other side of the locked gate, studying each unique handmade flower attached to the fence just above my head, out of reach. I pulled my phone out and started taking piles of pictures. I read the sign on the gate: La Plaza Cultural.[8] And I felt like I had found my garden, the one that understood me, the one that took trash and made it into a treasure.

I thought the bus ride was going to be longer. We stood on top of the Mount of Olives and took a group picture overlooking the city of Jerusalem, and Joav, our tour guide, taught us about the ancient city of David. A man with a camel kept trying to get us to ride it, and another guy with silver necklaces wove in and out of our group trying to sell his goods.

We finished up at the overlook and got back on the bus, immediately looking for our "bus buddies." It was a system set up on day one of the trip—everyone pick a person and each time we get on the bus, make sure your buddy is on there too. Most people, upon entering the bus and finding their seat, just did hand signals or looked around, but for me and my bus buddy, it was different. Every time we were told to check, I hollered, "BYRON!" and Byron yelled, "ANNIE!" It probably made the rest of our team crazy, but Byron didn't get left in Israel at any point, and neither did I. So. Success.

We started to drive, and just a few minutes later the driver pulled over again, and we all hopped out, headed to the garden of Gethsemane. *Right here?* I thought. *But we're right by the city of Jerusalem.*

I think in my mind, *The garden where Jesus prayed and suffered before being arrested was far out of town.* I pictured this secluded garden, miles from the action. And yet here we were, literally yards from the walls of Jerusalem, in this little patch of nature.

Joav spoke to us for a few minutes, reminding us what historians believe happened right where we were standing. And then he gave us some time to walk around the garden and think and pray.

I walked around for a few minutes, then eventually stopped and stood on the western side of the garden. It's blocked off by metal fencing and a half wall made of cement and bricks. I leaned up against the bricks and set my Bible on the cement ledge, just at the height of my hips. I turned to Matthew 26, the story that happened right in this very garden.

> *Then Jesus went with his disciples to a place called Gethsemane, and he said to them, "Sit here while I go over there and pray." He took Peter and the two sons of Zebedee along with him, and he began to be sorrowful and troubled. Then he said to them, "My soul is overwhelmed with sorrow to the point of death. Stay here and keep watch with me."*
>
> *Going a little farther, he fell with his face to the ground and prayed, "My Father, if it is possible, may this cup be taken from me. Yet not as I will, but as you will."*

Then he returned to his disciples and found them sleeping. "Couldn't you men keep watch with me for one hour?" he asked Peter. "Watch and pray so that you will not fall into temptation. The spirit is willing, but the flesh is weak."

He went away a second time and prayed, "My Father, if it is not possible for this cup to be taken away unless I drink it, may your will be done."

When he came back, he again found them sleeping, because their eyes were heavy. So he left them and went away once more and prayed the third time, saying the same thing.

Then he returned to the disciples and said to them, "Are you still sleeping and resting? Look, the hour has come, and the Son of Man is delivered into the hands of sinners. Rise! Let us go! Here comes my betrayer!"—Matthew *26:36–46* NIV

These verses, in my Bible, spread over two pages. The first paragraph sits on the bottom of the left page, and the rest is the top of the right page. I read these verses over and over again as the tears puddled in my eyes. I stopped reading and just started to rub my hands over the words and talk to Jesus. It was here, I just kept thinking, in this spot where He decided I was worth the sacrifice. It was here that He made the actual decision—I am saved right now because He was willing right here. If I can't hug Him and thank Him face-to-face, I will rub the pages where His name and suffering sit and pray my guts out in thankfulness.

The tears wouldn't stop. I'm such an emoter that I kept telling myself to dry it up and calm down, but after two or three minutes, I gave in to it. I decided to let my heart break. I had felt this before. Heartbreak has happened a time or two in my life, but this was different.

I felt His kindness.

And His kindness toward me in this place, in my sin, needing salvation, broke my heart.

I stood there crying for a lot of minutes. I just let the tears fall as long as they needed to, knowing I may never stand in that spot again. My soul, my insides, my guts needed to say all the things my mouth didn't know how to say. So I cried, I ran my fingers across the words of this story over and over again, and I whispered, "Thank You, thank You, thank You."

I turned and faced Jerusalem. There it was, just across the street. And my mind blinked back to that garden on 9th and Avenue C in New York City. And I understood Jesus better in that second than I ever had.

He was a city guy who loved a little piece of nature. Just like me and my walk around the East Village. He went looking for lovely in Jerusalem and ended up, repeatedly the Scriptures tell us, at the garden of Gethsemane. In fact, Luke 22:39 says that Jesus went out "as usual" to the Mount of Olives, where the garden is located. Looking at Jerusalem's wall, just over there from where I stood, I saw a side of Jesus I had never seen—the part of Him that sought out beauty, just as I do. The part of Him that found rest in nature, that part of Him that may have also been drawn to La Plaza Cultural and the long branches of the weeping willow. I'm like that too. The part of Him that loved the city but just needed some alone time, time away, outside of the city, to pray and remember why He loved the city in the first place.

What is it about a garden that draws us in, people like you and me and Jesus? Particularly, what is it about tiny grassy knolls in the center of town or community-grown plots of land or moments of nature just outside the hustle of the city?

I've found my garden in Nashville too. And it has absolutely changed my life.

LOOK FOR LOVELY

Take a walk today. Maybe it's just around the block, or maybe go to the local mall and take a few laps. While you are walking, look around. What do you see? What is catching your eye? Pray as you walk, asking God to direct your eyes to the things He doesn't want you to miss.

Think about Jesus. Even He, King of the Universe, needed to find rest. Do you have a quiet place you can go and be with the Father? Have you carved out time in your packed schedule lately just to be with Him? To let tears flow freely and experience His kindness? Remember, your time with Him isn't something to check off your to-do list. Do you love Him? Do you want to be in His presence? The more you spend time with Him, the more you'll want to spend time with Him. It's lovely how that works. And if there's anything you want to collect for this life of lovely you're building, it's a love relationship with the sweetest Man to ever walk this planet.

When You Find Lovely

I recently had two stress fractures in my right foot. I don't really know when the incident happened that brought them about, but alas, they were there. I'm prone to injury, which is why I pay for health insurance. It's not that I'm all that clumsy—well, maybe I am—but I do get hurt a lot. Knock on wood, my immune system is pretty strong after spending five years teaching in the public school system, so I don't often get sick. But injuries? I catch them all the time. Or drop them on my foot or trip over them.

After being in pain for a few weeks, I finally went to the doctor. And as he pushed on the swollen spot outside of my foot, like squeezing a trigger on a water gun, the tears rushed out. He patted my knee, told me we had some fractures, and gave me a plastic boot. (Well, I bought a plastic boot, but the bill didn't come for a week or so, so I walked out with it like it was a gift.) It really messed up my mojo and took away one of the things I love most: time at Radnor Lake.

➤———➤

My obsession started a few years ago. It was the week of my thirty-fourth birthday, and my family was in town to celebrate. My parents had recently gotten on a hiking kick, so they asked if there was somewhere around my house where we could hike. I called my old roommate Laura. She had told me how she met friends to hike sometimes, and so I thought she would be the one to help me out with a local hiking spot.

"Radnor Lake," her text read. "It is the best." And then she gave me directions on how to get there and where to park and what trails to do with my family. And we followed her directions completely. It was a beautiful walk, not too difficult but good exercise. We saw tiny baby deer and mama deer. We saw a couple of turkeys—WILD TURKEYS!—and we were merely ten minutes outside of the big city.

It was beautiful and fun, and I absolutely loved it.

I've long found nature to be a place where I connect with God. The mountains at sunrise. The beach at sunset. It can all leave me speechless with its beauty. But for some reason I had never connected hiking with beauty—probably because I considered it exercise—and as you know, exercise, traditionally, was no fun for me.

But, surprising even myself, I had such a good time walking the trails with my family that I decided to go back the next week. Just me.

I parked and walked up to the map of the trails right at the entrance of the lake trail, and because I so fear getting lost (it's a skill I have, leaving a place and never knowing how to get back from whence I came), I took lots of pictures of the map. I wanted to walk the same path my family and I had done the week before. My body was unhealthy and didn't want to exercise, but I had sniffed out what felt like something lovely with my family, and it was worth circling around again to see if I was right.

The fishermen in Jesus' time worked like this, eyes wide open to little glimmers of hope. In fact, when we meet Peter, he is doing this one particular type of fishing using an amphiblestron net. (I mean, no WAY did they call it that, right? Such a hard word. But that's the modern translation for us English speakers.) This kind of net is used in the shallower water and held in the hands of the fisherman. The edges of the nets are weighted so that when the net is thrown in the water, it will sink to the bottom, catching everything in that area. The fisherman then tightens the string he never threw out, and it collects together the edges of the net, closing it in on the fish in the middle.

Peter didn't just throw the net haphazardly, tossing it out and bringing it in over and over all day long. He would stand still and quiet in the more shallow parts of the Sea of Galilee, with its rocky and muddy bottom, and watch intently. When he saw a shimmering fish swim by, he knew there were probably more around. So that would be the cue to throw the net, hoping that by seeing one fish and trying to catch it, he would run into an entire school.

That's how I felt going back to Radnor. I had seen one little shimmering hope of joy found in exercise, and so I wanted to throw out my net and see if there was more to be caught there.

I started going once a week or so, listening to preaching podcasts on my walk every day. I would find one about forty-five minutes long, and if I pressed play right when I began on the wood chip-covered path, I would finish by the time I made the loop and got back to my car. It wasn't long before I wanted to go twice a week, just to be outside. And I started to see that my heart loved being at Radnor Lake, but so did my body. It was just a matter of weeks before I was finishing that trail quicker than the forty-five-minute podcasts. I would sit in my silver Toyota Camry and listen to the last few minutes of the podcast, wondering what in the world happened differently this particular time that made it so there were minutes left on the podcast.

(Um, Annie? You're getting stronger and faster. Yahoo.)

The map showed me there were "medium" and "difficult" trails all around Radnor Lake, and so far I had just done "easy." So on a Wednesday in the fall, I decided to try the "medium" trail.

I cannot put into words what a big deal this was for me (clearly, I'm going to try). For a quitter, for someone who traditionally has hated exercise and found no beauty in it at all, I was surprised at myself. Whatever I caught that first time walking at Radnor gave me the strength to want to do more, to throw out my net again, to challenge myself more, and to walk farther.

Because I had never thought about it, and because I had never really made the choice to persevere when things got hard, I had never experienced this emotion—the feeling of someone who finished one thing that was hard, so she pushed herself to try something even more difficult. (To be fair to myself, I've probably done that in some arenas before but certainly not in personal exercise or how I treated my body.)

The first day on the medium trail was *so* hard. The hills were serious, and the path was long. I looked at a map before heading out—even took a new picture of it with my phone, just focusing on this particular "medium" path. My earbuds in, I walked on the dirt path for ten to fifteen minutes, thinking, praying, processing. Two particular situations were in my mind—the first an invitation I had received to speak at an event, and the second had to do with a single man in my life. Neither had a clear right or wrong answer to me. Both were opportunities, options, chances that might be worth taking. I rolled them around in my head like marbles bouncing with each step I took.

I was worried, though. I was worried that I was going to miss what God had for me because I couldn't see the RIGHT or WRONG of the situations. "Just show me, Lord," I said, "and I'll do what You want. I just don't know where either of these is going."

I suddenly looked down and realized I did not know where I was, and I was pretty sure I was going the wrong way. Since I had never been here, I didn't know if I had possibly (GOD FORBID) hopped onto the "difficult" trail, or if I had somehow made a wrong turn. Everywhere I looked was brown path and green trees and dark shadows. Frustration crept up my back and pushed on my shoulders as I realized I was feeling that kind of confusion in lots of areas of my life—particularly those two situations that I couldn't get out of my brain and here, on this path. A little lost, a little sure I was wrong, a little concerned that I had missed the right thing.

I also thought, *I may be lost in these woods.*

When in a blink, God stamped a statement onto my heart. TRUST THE PATH.[9]

I looked down at my feet, at the path, and I realized what I knew was true—the path would take me back to the road eventually. I had seen it on the map, I knew I wasn't the first to do it, and the way the path was created, it ended at the road, a few hundred yards from the parking lot.

TRUST THE PATH, I heard God say. And I knew He didn't just mean the "medium" difficulty one at Radnor Lake. He meant the questions in my heart, the things I wonder about, the worries that I am going to miss Him. I don't have to know where things are going; I don't have to know the destination; I just have to trust the path.

Truth is, you probably DO NOT KNOW the destination. (I usually don't either, to be fair.) Am I right? Maybe you've changed your major five times already. Maybe you're taking a year off before starting college because you just don't know the RIGHT answer. Are you waiting for God to show up? Are you waiting for a pillar of cloud in the sky? He's saying TRUST THE PATH. Take that next step and then the next, and eventually, sooner or later, the path becomes clear.

Maybe Peter had similar moments throughout his journey when he had to go back to what he knew, the moment Jesus said the words, "Follow Me." He didn't know what was coming next; he just had to trust that those sandals on the path in front of him were leading to a good place. So while there were moments in his life of following Christ that were hard for Peter, he could go back to that moment and trust the One who is sovereign over the path before him.

God has repeatedly shown up for me like that at Radnor Lake. It feels like our place now. It's not just the beauty of the changing leaves; it's what He whispers to me around every corner. It's the joy I felt from Him when the medium path got too easy and I decided, after a year of walking, that the difficult path might be worth a try. It doesn't feel like God cares about my changing body or my strengthening leg muscles as much as He cares that my heart has gotten stronger and my resolve has changed.

Radnor Lake helped me quit quitting.

One day, walking the medium path at Radnor, I listened to a sermon about the secrets of a Spirit-filled life. As I huffed and puffed up the hills and around the curves of the trail, I agreed with all the preacher was saying and thought, *Yeah, I've got this stuff. I'm working it out.*

And then the last secret he said is, "Christians today need perseverance."

I stopped. My spirit immediately felt a catch. I lacked perseverance. I knew it. I knew I was broken. I knew the broken crazy had a purpose, and I realized this was it. I was learning to persevere, as I was learning to craft this life of lovely. The longer I looked for lovely, the more I kept going, the less I quit. But I had to keep choosing to persevere. Just as it says in Romans 5, I could already see that in my little bit of walking the trails, the suffering had made me persevere, my character (and strength) had grown, and I had hope to keep going. God was showing me in nature, and in my body, what has always been true in my spirit—if I would choose to see it that way. He was literally changing me from the inside out.

I listened through that particular podcast sermon every day at Radnor for the next week.

Perseverance. It's the other side of the coin from grace, which if you remember is where we started this whole journey.

Grace and perseverance. I have learned that to be all grace is to be lazy but to be all perseverance is to be judgmental. A good balance of grace and perseverance pushes us forward without destroying our spirit when we don't meet a goal, and it continually brings us back to our goals, dreams, and desires in order to remember why we began, how far we have come to get here, and where we ultimately want to go. It gives us permission to not be perfect but to strive toward excellence.

I think Jesus would love Radnor Lake and the trails because it reminds me of His garden. Just outside of town, nature at it's best, a place where the connection to God is clear and constant.

And you should hear me as I get to my car every day now. I try to jog the last few minutes on the paved path heading back toward the parking lot, and as soon as my hand can touch any part of my car, I say out loud: "I didn't quit. I'm not a quitter. I'm a finisher."

Because that's never been true of me like it is now. I'm a finisher. I don't quit.

What has happened to me at Radnor Lake, each day's walk building something in my soul, has affected every area of my life. God has used that place as the incubator for my growth and change. My hunch that throwing out my amphiblestron net would catch me something beautiful was right, and it ended up filling my net to capacity and overflowing.

-Section 3-

When I Found Lovely

Perspective Shifts

When I was a senior in high school, I dove head first into being a scrapbook queen. I mean, I went to scrapbooking conventions, y'all. No joke. As a seventeen-year-old. (I was a funny kid.) But I wanted so badly to have a beautiful piece of art at the end of my senior year that would become an heirloom for myself and my family. I used my babysitting money to buy all the best products, like stickers and paper and interestingly shaped scissors and a CORNER ROUNDER because I was big-time. I realize in our days of Pinterest and Shutterfly that some of you reading this may not even understand these words. Paper scrapbooks that you put together with glue and tape and scissors? What are these things you speak of, Annie? It was a big deal, trust me. (I still have the high school scrapbook as proof.)

My mother has some photo albums from her high school and college days, and I would pore over them as a kid, trying to see the life of this adult woman who lived in my house with me, but to see her like me, as a teenager. I wanted to see her life before

I existed. I loved it. I was fascinated to stare at her friends, to read what people wrote to her in her yearbooks, to see the pieces of art she made for my grandparents. I loved getting to know her before she knew me. And as I entered into my senior year, I wanted to make a scrapbook like that for my kids someday. (Or, as the case may be, for me to go back and look almost twenty years later and laugh at many of my decisions, particularly when it came to how often I wore a ponytail. Dear Annie, WEAR YOUR HAIR DOWN SOMETIMES. Sheesh.)

Mom collected memories from her high school and college life. So the propensity to collect things is a little bit in me already. My grandfather, who passed away just a week shy of his 102nd birthday, was an absolute hoarder, so I know it's in my blood going back at least two generations.

That skill has actually turned out to be handy for me. But in the last few years, since the broken crazy, God has opened my eyes to all these little moments of lovely around me, the ones we've talked about here and so many more. Speaking at my home church's summer camp, dancing after dinner on the Sea of Galilee, praying on stage before the Q Conference in Boston.

It's not that my life is all that different; it's just that I see it differently. So it feels like a brand-new life. I know, I know. Dramatic pause and dramatic language, but I'm telling you, that is how I feel. I feel like since I gave honest words to the broken crazy and started to get healthy around it, God has shown up and walked me into more healing than I even knew to ask for. And in it, He is opening my eyes.

And as I'm collecting these moments that matter, I'm actually just seeing more of Him. Because in the end that's what this is all about. When you find Jesus, you have found lovely. He is everything we need.

How I long for you to grasp that, to lay your life's foundation on it. Remember that house we talked about at the start of this journey back in Section 1? The one you're building? I don't know what you're envisioning, but that house may never have the white picket fence or open-concept kitchen or whatever else you've pinned on your dream house Pinterest board. But if you can get this one thing in place, trust me, you'll find that life of lovely you desire. Not a life free of pain, but one that knows the path to the One who will carry you through.

In the hallway of my house sits a Rubbermaid container of every journal I've ever written in. Upon my death, hopefully many years from now, those journals are to be burned, not read. My small group girls know this; all my friends know this. But for me this box of journals is an amazing collection of moments.

I pulled out the journal from while I was writing *Let's All Be Brave*, right as the broken crazy got real, and it's an absolute mess with barely any words—tons of skipped lines and empty pages and random doodles and a few words here and there about what was breaking my heart. It's a little hard to read because I can still feel some of those pains, but it's a collection, for me, of moments I need never to forget. Yes, I'm a different woman now, but I respect that woman who was suffering and how she didn't give up as much as she could have.

I decided I wanted an actual jar, just as a little reminder of some moments that I want to put all in the same place, particularly the ones I have written about here. I printed out that picture from Tel Aviv and slid it down the side of the jar, with my friends' faces outward. I snatched a blue paint chip and a yellow one from the local hardware store and I dropped them in there, thanking God again for Nichole. I took an older bottle of nail polish that I wasn't going to use anymore and let it settle to the bottom of the jar. I asked my counselor for her card at an appointment recently. She looked at me quizzically, but I told her I wanted it for my jar. So it's in there too. Connor gave me a baseball from a game I attended, so that sits on the bottom, rolled right to the middle. My friend who lost his wife in the accident? Her visitation pamphlet is in there, since her loss really was a catalyst for me understanding that sometimes the only beauty in anything, especially tragedy, is that Jesus is still on the throne. I grabbed a few fallen leaves as I walked the trails at Radnor Lake to add to the jar as well.

This journey itself, this book itself, in some crazy way, is a collection of what God has shown to be a life of lovely. When I found lovely, both in me and in the world, it changed everything.

Unfinished

I've lived in the same house in Nashville for the last six years. It's a rental, it's a fixer-upper, it's a mess. The basement floods when it rains, and the doors swell in the summers. But it's way cute and homey on the inside. It has plenty of space for living, and my small-group girls have always loved it. It's a really sweet and wonderful home.

In the front yard is a lamppost that looks just like the one from *The Lion, the Witch, and the Wardrobe*. It's alongside the driveway right in front of the house, but it's most often hidden by a massively overgrown bush that looks like a tree and also has a pretty solid helping of vines weaving around it.

The lamp stands just behind that mass of green, but "stands" is a bit of a generous descriptor. It leans. Depending on the season, the lamp can be leaning just a bit, or it can be almost touching the ground, like it did last winter when it snowed. It looked like the lamp bowed down under the power of the powder. There is a light bulb in the lamp, but it doesn't work.

And the lamp has six glass panes around it, but one is dangling off, and one is missing all together.

This is the reason my home is appropriately named Broke Lamp Manor. Because if you are looking for me, you'll find me at the house with the janky lamppost in the front yard.

If I'm honest, Broke Lamp Manor is a great name for my house because it is kind of who I am too. As much as I wish I could hide it, and as much as the rest of the house that is me can be cleaned up and a cute little place, you can't even get in the driveway without seeing the brokenness.

That's hard for me. I am one who would rather hide my brokenness, hide the lamp that is less than sufficient. But just like with my house, I feel God pushing me a bit to embrace my broken places and appreciate my weaknesses as much as I appreciate my strengths.

Throughout the time when this book was coming together, I wrestled with how to tie a nice, neat little bow on it so I could deliver a beautifully wrapped package to you. I struggled to finish because, honestly, I didn't feel like I was quite finished. I knew I wasn't the same Annie as when I started, but I wasn't perfect Annie either.

I still stand in front of the mirror at times and am totally mean with my words and my glare to every corner of my body. I ate a Butterfinger candy bar a few nights ago because I was scared, not hungry. I haven't exercised this week, and I haven't read my Bible like I want to. Because I have been traveling so much this month, I feel disconnected from my people, and overall I just kind of feel like a mess. I want to say I find beauty around every corner, but the truth is my eye is drawn to trash at times more than it is drawn to treasure.

I think often of Philippians 2:12 where it tells us to "work out" our salvation. And when I'm sitting across the table from one of my younger friends (Connor or Liz or April, for example), and we are talking about their faith questions or some struggle, I'm quick to remind them that no one is asking them to be done, no one expects perfection, and they shouldn't either. It's enough if they will just not give up and keep working out what God is doing on the inside. Trust the process, my counselor would say.

If perfection were the goal of this process, then it would make sense for me to feel like I had failed at this point. But perfection never was the goal. It was always perseverance. I'll admit I'm still working this out in my own life at times. I'm unfinished. And so are you.

There's this beautiful paradox in being humans. We are created in God's image, wonderfully made according to His plan, and He has never made a mistake. But you are still always a work in progress, never fully finished until that glorious day when we are in His presence and He truly and completely fixes all the broken places.

In the meantime, you persevere. You rejoice in who God made you to be, you face the hard places in life, and you walk forward in hope knowing what waits for you at the end of the road. We're always unfinished this side of heaven.

It's not a sprint; it's a marathon. We run. We stumble and fall. He picks us up again and again. It's like the words of one of my favorite hymns:

> *Pardon for sin and a peace that endureth,*
> *Thine own dear presence to cheer and to guide,*
> *Strength for today and bright hope for tomorrow—*
> *Blessings all mine, with ten thousand beside.*
>
> *Great is Thy faithfulness!*
> *Great is Thy faithfulness!*
> *Morning by morning new mercies I see.*
> *All I have needed Thy hand hath provided.*
> *Great is Thy faithfulness, Lord, unto me.*[10]

"Strength for today and bright hope for tomorrow." Yes! That just sums it up. You don't have to be perfect. You don't have to be finished. You don't have to know what tomorrow holds. Jesus gives you strength to endure today as you look with hope to the future. This life of lovely is a journey. And we know the very end, and it is beautiful.

Everyone's mentor Bob Goff reminded me once to be the same person on the surface that I am at the depths of me. My aunt and uncle lived on a lake that used to be a town in a valley. When they decided to dam off the river and fill the valley with water to create a man-made lake for energy production, all the people moved out of the town, but they didn't destroy the buildings.

It's so freaky. You can boat all summer long, and ski and such, and never have a problem, never experience anything except a fun day on the lake. But you have to be careful in the winter, when the water is down, because just twenty to thirty feet below the surface are the roofs of homes, and in the dead of winter, you can see the steeple of the church poking out of the center of the body of water. It's a dishonest lake, actually. It wants you to believe the water is pure and clean when actually there are algae-covered buildings just thirty feet below you.

As Bob and I talked about water and depth and what lies beneath, he said, "Annie, to be authentically you, you have to be the same at one foot of depth as you are at thirty."

At one foot? I'm finished. I'm shiny. I'm clean. I'm a great Annie.

At thirty feet? I'm still unfinished.

It feels freeing to say that. And freedom is incredibly beautiful.

For all this to matter to you and feel honest to me, I have to tell you what lies below the surface today. And so here is the thirty-feet-deep view that I'm going to work to show at one foot too:

I'm a different Annie than I used to be. I had to walk through the hard places to find the beauty. My cape of shame has long been trashed, and my days of constant self-hate have passed. What God has done in my heart and life (and body, to be honest) in the last few years, since the broken crazy, is nothing short of a miracle. I used to be a quitter; now I cross more finish lines than I ever have before. I didn't know what it felt like for my character to be stretched and grown, but I do now. I thought I understood hope, but the kind of hope that has become mine more recently is a treasure I don't want to release. I have surrounded myself with people who are for me, for my health, and for my sanity, and it has made for a tribe I am deeply grateful for and indebted to. I am growing and changing, and I like me more than I ever have.

And I am very unfinished. (I bet you are too.)

But I am very loved. (I know you are too.)

Epilogue

(I know. I'm not near fancy enough for an epilogue. It is something serious literary types do. I'm just Annie. But I had one more thing to say, and what do you do when you have one more thing to say? You epilogue.)

This Is My Song

Even when I had those two stress fractures in my right foot, I couldn't resist going to Radnor Lake to walk the trails. It was the first day of fall—not officially, just according to the cool weather—and so I just couldn't pass up the opportunity for the bright afternoon sun to warm me as that autumn breeze blew through the leaves and onto my skin as I walked around the lake.

A sermon was waiting for me in my podcast app, and some friends had told me it was a real doozie, a good one, so I was excited about that as well. I hadn't been on the trails in about a week, which for me is a long time, especially when the weather is gorgeous.

I walked slower than usual, giving myself permission to let up the normal speed since I had an actual injured foot. I also took the flat path, that first path I had ever walked, around toward my favorite #10 bench, as the pastor taught in my ears about 2 Chronicles 20 and the increase we all need of God's presence and God's victory.

I started to think about all the ways I had been looking for lovely. And the pastor began talking about 2 Chronicles 20:22.

As they began to sing and praise, the LORD set ambushes against the men of Ammon and Moab and Mount Seir who were invading Judah, and they were defeated.
—*2 Chronicles 20:22 NIV*

He said, "You see, when the word of the Lord does its full work in you and in me, there is a natural, normal response to God in song."

I'm not a great singer, but I resonated with what he was preaching. In fact, I almost felt like I could explode with YES and AMEN. God had done such a full and life-changing work in me those last few years, everything you've read so far here, that I felt like a song could burst out of me at any point. I began walking faster, I noticed mainly because my foot began to throb, and I turned the corner and dipped down that hill right by the little wooden bridge. The ground was soft because it had rained, but it wasn't muddy; it just gave a little under my steps.

As I listened, I told God I wanted to sing Him a song—I wanted a song that spoke to that season, to the healing He had done in me, to the work I knew He had completed in my heart.

What song did I want to sing to Him? There on the path, I started to think of you, and I started to think of what I would sing to you about Jesus if that wasn't a terrible idea for your ears. And here's what came to my mind:

I would sing that He is a miracle worker, even when you aren't seeing it. I'd sing that His love is unmatched, and you can see that best in the darkness. I'd sing that my life is only because of Jesus and only for Jesus, and the mess of an Annie I would be without Him is almost too painful for me to imagine. I'd sing over and over again that He knows me better than I know myself, and for all the hard days and all the confusing moments and all the pain I have faced, I wouldn't trade a minute of it because of how I know Him now. I'd share a verse about how He can be trusted, how God is your Father and Jesus is your best Friend and the Holy Spirit is here to comfort you.

I would sing that I know no greater joy than living life with Jesus, and I lack absolutely nothing because I have Him.

I'd cry when I sing it, like I cried when I thought it on the path around Radnor Lake, like I'm crying as I write. Because it's all been for this. It's all been because I want to know Jesus and I want you to know Jesus.

And as I continued to walk, in my headphones, Pastor Bill mentioned something about waking up singing a song. "Pay attention," he said. "God may be giving you the song for that next season."

And I froze. Right there across the bridge as the path pushed up a slight incline, I stopped trying to write the song about God I would sing for you, and I remembered that I woke up singing that morning.

I paused the podcast as I tried to remember and call back to my mind what I was singing when the sun shone through my eastern-facing bedroom window. I sang it for a while, just quietly to myself, as I made my bed and got going for the day. But what was it? I was spinning through all the memories of my day, willing the lyrics to come back to me.

I knew I needed to remember. Because I knew, right there on the path, that I was supposed to go on this walk this day, to hear this podcast, to remember the words I woke up singing, for God to give me the song for my next season. No wonder I couldn't get Radnor off my mind that morning, even with the stress-fractured foot and a bit of a glitch in my calendar that got me to the lake later than I usually go. The whispers of the Holy Spirit, pointing me toward that walk, are clear to me now. But I was dying to remember what the song was!

I started walking again, hoping my mind would bring it back to the front as I knew it was the Holy Spirit reminding me of the song that morning.

Oh yes!, I thought as it finally came to me. *I played the song when I got to the office this morning. "We Dance."* I still didn't remember the exact lyrics, but I remembered the song. It's a deep cut from the *You Make Me Brave* worship album. I finished the last ten minutes of the podcast sermon, and as I crossed over the lake on the metal bridge, the podcast ended, and I scrolled through my music to "We Dance."

Tears poured as I heard the lyrics I woke up singing that very morning . . .

And I will lock eyes with the One who's ransomed me,
the One who gave me joy for mourning.
And I will lock eyes with the One who's chosen me,
the One who set my feet to dancing.[11]

And don't you know that's exactly my story. That's 100 percent who I am today and where I am today.

He ransomed me. Jesus paid for me with His life so that I would belong to no one else. Even if the deal didn't come with the promise of eternity, which it does, I would take it and be deeply grateful because He has made my life worth living.

And I want, more than anything else, to lock eyes with this God who has taken my mourning and turned it into joy. When I persevered, when I hung on through the pain, when I willingly handed Him my hurts from over the years and the new ones birthed, He gave me joy, the difference in size like a watermelon seed of mourning to a massive colorful watermelon of joy.

And He set my feet to dancing. The girl who was too insecure to let loose on the dance floor, the one who felt too heavy to move with grace or ease, the one who has had to push through the hurt and the fear to a place of freedom? God set her feet, my feet (even the fractured one), to dancing.

Maybe that's the moral of this whole thing. Maybe the most beautiful thing we can look at, in order to persevere, finish, thrive, live, is the eyes of our God. So if you need me, that's where I hope you always find me. Locking eyes with the One who has chosen me.

And so I leave you with that. I want you to look for this life of lovely and find it. I want you to resolve to be the kind of woman who does not quit, who does not give up, who strengthens your mind and heart to let the work God is doing in you come to completion.

This is my story.

This is my song.

Praising my Savior all the day long.

Thank You

Thanks to you, my sweet reader friend, for meeting me here. I love writing for you and being friends with you. It matters. Live that life, that life of lovely. Don't apologize for it or run from it—live it. My prayers are with you. For real.

Thank you to B&H, Michelle, Jana, and Mary for making this book a reality and loving the next generation with the biggest hearts. It matters.

To my team at Downs Books Inc. I love love love working with y'all and can't imagine a better group of humans to have around me.

To teenage Annie: I'm thinking of you in this one. I know it was hard; I remember it well. I think this book is a gift from me to you, a reminder of how I honor your pain and worries and struggles, but don't live there anymore. Healing is coming, sister.

God, You are kinder than I ever knew. Thank You for loving me through every season, for walking so close to me in my story, and for making my life more lovely than I could have ever dreamed. I'm thankful for the love of the Father, the sacrifice of Jesus, and the comfort of the Holy Spirit.

Notes

1. Annie F. Downs, *Let's All Be Brave* (Grand Rapids, MI: Zondervan, 2014).

2. For deeper study, see Psalm 139:13–14, Ephesians 2:10, and Isaiah 45:12.

3. See Christopher Bergland, "Why Do the Songs From Your Past Evoke Such Vivid Memories?" *Psychology Today*, December 11, 2013, https://www.psychologytoday.com/blog/the-athletes-way/201312/why-do-the-songs-your-past-evoke-such-vivid-memories.

4. Ernie Rettino and Debbie Kerner Rettino, "Cares Chorus" *Psalty's Funtastic Praise Party*, accessed October 4, 2018, http://www.psalty.com/track/689448/cares-chorus?feature_id=140960.

5. Author wrote a similar chapter entitled "Mango-Colored Nail Polish" in *180: Stories of People Who Changed Their Lives by Changing Their Minds* (Kansas City, MO: The House Studio, 2010).

6. See "Claude Monet's Home in Giverny," Monet's House, Giverny and Vernon: In the Heart of Impressionism, accessed October 4, 2018, http://giverny.org/monet/home.

7. See "Exhibitions and Events," MoMA, accessed October 4, 2018, http://www.moma.org/visit/calendar/exhibitions/963.

8. See "La Plaza Cultural de Armando Perez Community Garden," accessed October 4, 2018, http://laplazacultural.com/#1.

9. Author also wrote a version of this for (in)Courage. See Annie F. Downs, "Trust the Path," (in)Courage, accessed October 4, 2018, http://www.incourage.me/2014/09/trust-the-path.html.

10. Thomas O. Chisholm and William M. Runyan, "Great Is Thy Faithfulness" (Carol Stream, IL: Hope Publishing Co., 1923, 1951).

11. Steffany Gretzinger and Amanda Falk, "We Dance" (Redding, CA: Bethel Music Publishing, 2014), https://bethelmusic.com/albums/you-make-me-brave.

CHECK OUT THE NEW SEASON OF *THAT SOUNDS FUN* ON THE
RELEVANT PODCAST NETWORK. IF IT SOUNDS FUN TO ANNIE,
YOU'RE GOING TO HEAR ABOUT IT.

Other B&H books from Annie F. Downs

A LIFE OF LOVELY JOURNAL

LOOKING FOR LOVELY   **REMEMBER GOD**

ANNIEFDOWNS.COM/BOOKS/